BEHIND THE SMILE

BEHIND THE SMILE

The Heartbreaking Journey of Raising a Son with Addiction and Mental Illness

DIANA WARD

O'LEARY PUBLISHING
The Influencer's Press

NAPLES, FL

Copyright © 2024 by Diana Ward
All rights reserved.

Published in the United States by
O'Leary Publishing
www.olearypublishing.com

The views, information, or opinions expressed in this book are solely those of the authors involved and do not necessarily represent those of O'Leary Publishing, LLC.

The author has made every effort possible to ensure the accuracy of the information presented in this book. However, the information herein is sold without warranty, either expressed or implied. Neither the author, publisher, nor any dealer or distributor of this book will be held liable for any damages caused either directly or indirectly by the instructions or information contained in this book. You are encouraged to seek professional advice before taking any action mentioned herein.

All rights reserved. No part of this book may be reproduced or transmitted in any form by any means, electronic, mechanical, photocopy, recording, or other without the prior and express written permission of the author, except for brief cited quotes.

For information on wholesale orders or getting permission for reprints and excerpts, contact: O'Leary Publishing at admin@olearypublishing.com

ISBN: 978-1-952491-68-9 (print)
ISBN: 978-1-952491-69-6 (ebook)
Library of Congress Control Number: 2023920613

Developmental Editing by Heather Davis Desrocher
Line Editing by Jennifer Doody
Proofreading by Kat Langenheim
Cover and interior design by Jessica Angerstein

Printed in the United States of America

If you or someone you know
is struggling with suicidal thoughts
or mental illness, please see the resource list
at the back of the book.

CONTENTS

Foreword i
Preface: The Unthinkable 1
Chapter 1 ♥ Becoming a Mother 5
Chapter 2 ♥ Family of Four 13
Chapter 3 ♥ Losing Myself 21
Chapter 4 ♥ Figuring it Out 29
Chapter 5 ♥ Starting Over 39
Chapter 6 ♥ Dancing for Happiness 49
Chapter 7 ♥ Crossfaded 55
Chapter 8 ♥ Hope and Disappointment 63
Chapter 9 ♥ Searching for Cody 73
Chapter 10 ♥ A Mother's Hope 81
Chapter 11 ♥ Grandma Penny 89
Chapter 12 ♥ Letting Go 95
Chapter 13 ♥ The Longest Flight 103
Chapter 14 ♥ Grief – What I Did Not Know 117

Afterward 127
Acknowledgments 131
Reflections 133
Resources 135
About the Author 137

FOREWORD

For whatever reason you picked up this book, you will not regret it. As an executive for a psychiatric hospital in southwest Florida, where we treat adults for acute mental illness and substance use disorders, I am fortunate to know and work closely with Diana Ward. She is a hero in my eyes. There isn't anyone I know with more personal experience and professional qualifications to shed light on the challenges associated with a loved one who is battling addiction or mental illness.

Diana knows firsthand the frustration and pain of watching a loved one navigate struggles with addiction and mental illness. She is exactly who you would hope to work with as a patient or family member navigating this process. Her compassion and empathy for those in her presence are admirable, and she is an advocate for hope and healing regardless of the situation.

Life has an interesting way of wiring us for what we are called to do, but sometimes it can feel overwhelming. As Diana journeyed through life with young children, marriage, and financial struggles, the punches kept coming. She often felt inadequate and ill-equipped to manage her son's behavioral issues. Maybe you can relate to feeling ill-equipped or inadequate to conquer the challenges of your life? Finding answers can be like trying to find a needle in a haystack.

Diana is a beautiful soul determined to share the silver lining of her worst nightmare. In *Behind the Smile*, Diana shares with you her journey as a mother of a son who battled his demons for the better part of his life. Sadly, addiction and mental illness know no limitations and they certainly do not discriminate. This book will show you that you are not alone in the fight.

Amber Hentz, MHA
CEO of Park Royal Behavioral Health Services

PREFACE
THE UNTHINKABLE

This life is a journey of learning and experiencing all things – as is this book. Twenty-two years of joy, sadness, frustration, anger, love, loss, and most importantly, learning – that is what I experienced with my son. I learned many things from Cody, especially absolute patience. How powerful to accept others as they are – with their flaws and their individual beauty. I learned not to force others into the box where I think they should fit.

I also learned to be unapologetically myself – not to change for others, and not to feel ashamed of being different or not living up to other's expectations. I learned resilience. There were times I wanted to give up on Cody, and on myself. I wanted to give up being a mother. But I became resilient – and in that resiliency I learned to trust myself and find ways to help him. I threw out every conventional way of mothering, of disciplining, of teaching a child. I learned how to allow life to flow, instead of forcing it to be the way I thought it should be.

I also learned that in death, there is a rebirth – a new way of living. While the birthing process is painful, there is a beauty in it. We must find beauty – even when it seems difficult or impossible to find. I promise you, it is there. I have learned to look deeply, and to look long. In looking, I have found happiness again, and a reason for living.

I am on this earth to share my son's story of mental illness, addiction and suicide; and to help educate people about what the depths of despair really look like from a mother's perspective. This is the story of mothering a child tormented by mental illness – a child who self-medicated himself into psychosis in his search for the meaning of life. This is the story of a mother's love, grief and awareness – a story that many others share. To all those whose loved ones struggle with mental illness or addiction: I see you. I hear you. I love you. I know sharing this story will give hope to other parents who have lost a child. May this book offer understanding, comfort, and hope that we can have both grief and joy in life.

This is a story about life and death, living and loss, grief and acceptance. It is the story of a life, the life of my son Cody, who was known for his captivating smile. This reminds us that many who live with mental illness or addiction hide behind the smile – behind a mask of "everything is good." The smile or mask is often only a facade hiding the demons they fight daily.

This book is also a celebration of Cody's life and a tribute to the beautiful human that he was. As I continue to grapple with the grief of his life ending, I think back to how his life began.

In Loving Memory of my son,
Cody Howard Ward (1999-2021),
and to all mothers who have lost a child.

CHAPTER 1
BECOMING A MOTHER

January 18th, 1999
Monday, 9:00 p.m.
Las Vegas, Nevada

It was the end of the day. My husband, Richard, was brushing his teeth, and I was just getting ready for bed. I felt a balloon pop inside of my body and a gush of warmth between my legs. I told my husband, "I think my water just broke..." There were no contractions and no pain, but I shook uncontrollably and I went into shock. It was surreal – I almost felt like I had an *out of body* experience. I was also excited. I knew my baby boy was coming into this world!

My pregnancy had been a good one with no complications – I never even threw up. I was pretty nauseous in the first trimester, but that was it; the rest had been a piece of cake. I felt great, and only gained about 25 pounds. I had worked out during the entire pregnancy and did not consume anything harmful – not even caffeine. At the time, I was a practicing Latter Day Saint (Mormon). It was against our faith to drink alcohol or hot caffeinated beverages, or anything else that was harmful to the body, which was considered a *temple*.

When we arrived at the hospital I was four centimeters dilated. I would have to wait for an epidural, which is only given after five centimeters because it slows down the contractions.

For the next few hours I experienced waves of contractions. As each one began, I would tense up and squeeze the bar on the hospital bed. But then I focused on breathing through the contractions to lessen the pain. My focal point was a picture on the wall. I do not recall what was in the picture specifically as I was in so much pain; but the focal point, along with the breathing, helped me resist the urge to tense up. It really did work. As any woman who has ever been in labor knows, it requires intense focus, and I did not want anyone touching or talking to me. I needed all my attention on laboring. It was a real relief when the doctor gave me the epidural and I felt nothing!

CHAPTER 1

Once I had been poked, prodded and checked *down there* so many times, I was over any embarrassment and did not really care who was there – at least as far as females. My older sister, Richard, and his mother were all there for the birth. My parents were not. When I had announced that I was marrying Richard and converting to the Mormon faith, my parents pretty much disowned me. They did not support my marriage and definitely did not support me leaving the Catholic faith to become a Mormon. They did not come to my wedding and were not there for the birth of my son. Luckily, Richard's parents were extremely loving and supportive of me and so I had a family.

Tuesday, 6:32 a.m.

Cody Howard Ward was born into this world weighing 6.1 pounds. He arrived screaming and absolutely beautiful. This polarity would prove to continue throughout his life. He did not have any hair on his head, but he did have lanugo all over his body. He was red and skinny but perfect in my eyes. I did not grow up around babies, and as the youngest in the family I was rarely around them. My mother-in-law helped me a lot and showed me how to get him to nurse. He did not seem interested and would not latch on, but at the time, I did not think anything of it. He was so little.

The whole birthing process is quite a shock to the body – and then you are left to care for a little human. The morning after Cody was born, I was so anxious I got out of the hospital bed and began cleaning the hospital room.

My family thought I was crazy; but I am not the best patient and do not like someone taking care of me. The nurse came in to take my son to be circumcised, and Richard went with Cody. It was extremely quick, and when they brought him back I took my son in my arms and looked down at his little hands and fingernails. I started crying thinking how traumatic it was to cut the skin off of his penis! I contemplated why we even do that in our culture and wondered if I should have agreed to it. I didn't want him growing up and feeling *different*, but later I would find out how different he was regardless of whether or not he was circumcised!

After 24 hours we left the hospital to take our baby home. On the drive home, Cody started screaming hysterically. *What was wrong?* "Pull over!" I told Richard. I took Cody out of the car seat and held him but he wouldn't stop screaming. We were new parents, and not knowing what to think or do Richard suggested checking his diaper. Sure enough, he had pooped! I changed his diaper and we were back on the road. This intense crying was the first sign of how sensitive Cody was to the environment around him.

CHAPTER 1

Cody would not breastfeed. He would not latch on to my nipple and I panicked at the thought that he was not getting enough nutrition. I knew if I was stressed Cody could feel that, and it would not be healthy for him. So I gave up breastfeeding and fed him formula from a bottle.

After each and every formula feeding Cody would projectile vomit. I went through a lot of burp rags, towels, and blankets, as well as outfits, daily.

Feeding Cody was a challenge, but so was getting him to stay asleep. *Any* noise would wake him. He would open his eyes with a startled look on his face and scream. I had to turn off the phone (a landline back then) and hope that no one would come to the door, or that the dog wouldn't bark.

As if that was not enough, Cody needed to be held all of the time. If I put him down in a crib or bassinet he would scream (which created more stress for me). I could not get anything done, let alone sleep.

I was exhausted and my baby was not at peace at all. *Was this normal? Was I just a bad mother? Was I just not cut out to be a mother?*

Everybody else seemed to just blow it all off, so maybe I was just being paranoid as a new mother. I felt disheartened. All my other friends had happy babies who slept through the night and breastfed so easily. The other mothers were glowing and seemed delighted to be mothers. I felt inadequate.

When I saw my doctor, I mentioned that I felt anxious all of the time. He told me that I had postpartum depression and prescribed Zoloft. I was confused.

I said, "But I'm not depressed Doc."

He said, "Postpartum depression also includes anxiety."

Again, I felt like a failure of a mother. Receiving a diagnosis like that made me feel like I was not meant to be a mother. I felt ashamed. *Why am I not enjoying being a mother and why do I have to take medications for this? What is wrong with me?*

I would try to get him to sleep by singing, "You are my sunshine, my only sunshine. You make me happy when skies are gray. You'll never know, dear, how much I love you. Please don't take my sunshine away."

After three months I finally had a rhythm and routine with Cody. I thought, *Okay, I got this. I can handle this. I know what he wants when he fusses and we seem to have a bond now.* But, every evening around 5:00 pm, Cody would go into an inconsolable screaming rage. It was like clockwork. I would sing to him, bounce him, and walk around with him – but nothing worked. This happened *everyday*. Everyone said he was just *colicky*.

CHAPTER 1

Colicky: *experiencing or denoting severe pain in the abdomen (colic) due to gas or intestinal obstruction*

We tried different brands of formula, and ended up with the most expensive one in hopes of giving our baby some relief. Nothing worked. Eventually, Richard and I took turns walking him and bouncing him. Usually, after three hours, Cody would finally stop screaming.

I was not convinced it was colic, but there really was nothing else we could do. Eventually we gave him an antacid and continued to feed him the expensive formula. But deep inside I felt like something else was going on with Cody because he was so sensitive to his environment. He would scream if he was too hot, or too cold, or if it was too loud. It was difficult to take him anywhere, especially a loud restaurant because he would scream. Typically one of us would have to leave the restaurant during the meal so we would not disturb the rest of the restaurant.

Again, I asked myself, *Is this normal?* My gut said no. I wanted nothing more than to be a good mom and to make my baby happy. I gave Cody my heart and soul then and for the next 22 years, but was only able to help him have fleeting moments of happiness.

Our life was about to get more complicated. Twelve weeks after Cody was born I missed my period and felt *off*. I took a pregnancy test and it was positive. This was not planned, and I was not happy.

Later that night I asked Richard if we could go out to dinner because I had something important to tell him. I handed him the pregnancy stick that said, "Positive."

He looked at it and I started crying. Not a happy cry. A sad cry. I did not want another baby. I wasn't good at mothering the one I had. My baby boy seemed miserable and so was I! I was just starting to bond with my son, and he demanded so much attention and energy. All I could think was, *How in the hell am I supposed to take care of another one, and so close together*!?

CHAPTER 2
FAMILY OF FOUR

December 3, 1999
Friday, 6:13 p.m.
Las Vegas, Nevada

Giving birth to two children in the same year (Irish Twins) was not easy. The two pregnancies were similar, and while I was not sick and the pregnancy went pretty smoothly, I was tired most of the time. Since most of my attention was going towards Cody, there was not much time to think about anything else.

The day Jessica was born, I went in for my check up with the obstetrician and I was dilated to three cm. He told me to walk around and then to go to the hospital. Richard and I went to a mall where I could walk around while Cody stayed with Richard's parents. I walked around for about two hours and even jogged up and down escalators. I felt no contractions or pain, and when I arrived at the hospital the nurse seemed skeptical, since I was calm and appeared not to be in any discomfort. But when she checked I was seven cm dilated (10 cm is ready to deliver). She was shocked and could not believe I felt no discomfort.

They rushed me into a room and offered me an epidural, which I accepted. My water had not broken yet so they broke it for me, and then my body went into shock and started shaking uncontrollably – just like it did during Cody's birth. Two hours later Jessica was born.

Jessica was healthy and beautiful. She weighed just under 7 pounds. She had a small amount of brown hair on her head and much more fat on her than Cody. She had some mucus in her lungs so they suctioned it out and put her on oxygen, but she was fine. I wanted to go home to enjoy my own birthday, and my doctor agreed. Thankfully, less than 24 hours later, I was discharged to go home.

Having two babies in less than a year was challenging to say the least. Jessica was the complete opposite in temperament from Cody. She breast fed with ease and slept well. She was calm and happy most of the time. The most challenging thing was that once Jessica was finally asleep,

Cody would scream. This wore me down and I longed for sleep, or even just some quiet. Richard helped out quite a bit in the evenings, but he was at work all day.

When they both began to crawl I felt like I was losing my mind. Imagine two babies in diapers and one taking a bottle and one breast feeding. How *the heck does someone juggle this?* Well somehow, someway, I did – but not with much grace.

One day, while Jessica was sleeping in the swing and Cody was playing in the toy room under the stairs, I noticed how quiet it was. It was too quiet. If he was quiet something was not right.

When I checked on him, there was something on his hands and all over the wall. *No, it can't be! No, no, no, no! Oh my gosh, it is poop!!!!* Cody had taken off his diaper and smeared his poop everywhere! I grabbed him and put him in the bath. Then I scrubbed the walls, the carpet, the toys, and everything that he had touched. I was at my wit's end and called his father, who was at work. "Come home right now!" I screamed, crying. "I can't take this anymore! I need help!"

This was an example of how sensitive Cody was to his environment. The feeling of poop next to his skin was unbearable to him. It also showed how curious he was about everything. Cody could not just sit still and observe.

He explored everything and used all his senses to take in his environment. This often gave him sensory overload, which led to meltdowns. His meltdowns included biting and scratching anyone within his reach – often his sister. On a daily basis Jessica would scream in pain. Once, she had a scratch down her face that was bleeding. She still has a scar on her face from Cody.

In an attempt to keep Cody occupied and give myself a break, I would take them to McDonald's playland. This gave me a chance to sit and eat in peace. Cody was occupied and mostly safe in a contained area. Unfortunately, if there were other children playing as well, it would not take long before one of them would come out of the slide screaming because Cody had bitten him. The child's mother would be upset. I would apologize profusely and then grab Cody and Jessica and leave. This happened numerous times at parks and other play areas. I could not take Cody anywhere without worrying that he would hurt another child.

None of this seemed normal to me. No other child that I knew acted this way. But when I would bring this up to family, friends, or professionals, I felt dismissed. Many would say, "Oh he's just a boy, he'll grow out of it."

Cody was a little blonde-haired, blue-eyed ball of energy climbing around the house like a monkey and he kept me on my toes. He was also an escape artist. I would put him in his car seat in the car, which had multiple connection points and fasteners, and I would look back only to find him completely out of his car seat! He had to be watched every second because he had so much energy. If I left him he might climb on top of a counter and end up in the cupboards in the bathroom or kitchen. Cody was an extremely light sleeper and required the perfect setting to sleep. Many times I would go for a drive just to get him to sleep. Once he was asleep I would pull over and sleep in the car myself. If I turned off the car and moved him, he would immediately wake up. As I felt like I was losing my mind I would look at my little boy and his beautiful smile and was reminded that it was all worth it.

Going to a restaurant, store, or even church proved to be the ultimate challenge. Cody did not like to be told *no* or have things taken away from him. In addition, changing settings would cause a meltdown. Leaving the park would cause a complete screaming meltdown that could last for hours. I often thought, there is no way this kid has any more energy to scream and cry; but sure enough, he kept going.

I cannot count the number of times I had a basket full of groceries that I just left because Cody was screaming. I received awful looks from people in the store and I knew they were thinking, *Can you just shut your kid up?*

Many people would say things like, "He just needs a good ass woopin." Trust me – if that would have helped him I would've done it. And don't think my husband and I didn't try *everything*. I tried ignoring, spanking, talking to, changing environments – you name it.

When Cody was 3 years old, we began using the time out method. If he bit someone or disobeyed us we put him in his room. He would scream for hours. This type of behavior never ended all the way through high school. The one thing I can say about Cody is he was relentless when he wanted something. He did not give up.

During this period, Cody spent a lot of time with his grandma Penny (Richard's mom). She adored her grandchildren and had a special bond with Cody. In order to try to make him happy she gave him what he would call "peese" (a sippy cup of milk with sugar added). He loved his "peese" and would fill up on it instead of food. Cody was very picky when it came to food. For years he only ate cereal and "eggies" with ketchup. I tried all types of food, but he would gag and spit them out.

Almost everyone – babysitters, family, friends – had a tough time handling Cody. Grandma Penny handled Cody pretty well and protected him fiercely anytime I tried to discuss his challenges. Whenever I needed a break, off to Grandma's he would go. I felt relaxed and confident that he was in good hands. Over the years Grandma was my saving grace; she and Cody had a special bond.

By the time Cody was 3 years old I was drained. The challenges we faced with Cody put a strain on our marriage. Of course, after Jessica was born, I swore I would never have another child. But something strange happened. I went on a women's retreat with my church up in the mountains, and while I was praying something hit me. *I want to have another baby*. It came out of nowhere. When I got home, I told Richard and he was elated – he always wanted a big family. So we began trying for a third child.

CHAPTER 3
LOSING MYSELF

June 24, 2003
Tuesday, 6:57 p.m.
Las Vegas, Nevada

Our third child, Savannah Zel, was born on a fine evening in June. We chose her middle name after her paternal great-grandmother, Zelma. She weighed the most out of all three of my children, coming in just under 8 pounds. She had the biggest blue eyes and a little blonde hair when she was born. She was the easiest of all three, sleeping through the night early on.

Having two toddlers was a handful, but having a third was nearly unmanageable, even though Savannah was a well-tempered child. I was a new, home real estate agent, so I took the maximum of twelve weeks for maternity leave. I breast fed her for twelve weeks and then introduced the bottle. All three children were in daycare when I worked because Richard ran his own pool maintenance company and was gone all day – sometimes for 12 hours.

Cody was 5 years old and in daycare when we learned that Cody had some major emotional and behavioral issues. We had noticed this at home, of course, but the true test was seeing him in a school setting outside of family and friends. One day we received a call from the daycare administrator that Cody had to be *restrained* due to a violent temper tantrum. The daycare attendant said she had to hold him for hours. This would happen any time Cody had to transition from one activity to another.

Sadly, none of this surprised me, but how should we handle this? Richard was furious that anybody would lay their hands on our son. But I understood that the teacher was attempting to prevent Cody from hurting himself or anyone else. When the school suggested we have him professionally evaluated by a psychiatrist, my heart sank. All my fears and intuition had been right – there was something wrong with my son. I began my internet search to find some answers about what was happening with my boy.

I searched for *sensitivity to light, sounds, hot and cold.* My results suggested Asperger's Syndrome (now considered to be on the autism spectrum). I had no psychology education at this time and did not understand what any of this meant. We had a psychiatrist evaluate him. The diagnosis was: Pervasive Development Disorder Not Otherwise Specified (PDD-NOS):

> PDD-NOS is characterized by delays in the development of socialization and communication skills. Parents may notice associated behaviors as early as infancy. These may include delays in using and understanding language, difficulty relating to people, unusual play with toys and other objects, difficulty with changes in routine or surroundings and repetitive body movements or behavior patterns... In addition, there is a high-functioning group (around 25 percent) whose symptoms largely overlap with that of Asperger Syndrome, but who differ in terms of having a lag in language development and mild cognitive impairment. (Asperger syndrome does not generally involve speech delay or cognitive impairment.) from autismspeaks.org

PDD did not explain all of Cody's symptoms and my gut told me it was more along the line of Asperger's Syndrome. PDD and Asperger's were new in the psychiatric field and many doctors were still unsure of how to diagnose Cody. He had all of the symptoms of Asperger's, which included repetitive behaviors, inability to identify emotional cues, difficulty in coping with emotional situations such as changes in patterns and becoming easily frustrated, abnormal responses to sensory stimuli, obsession or hyperfocus on one topic of interest.

Now that I had some information and knowledge, I reflected on Cody's behaviors. One thing he did was to put his hands in the air and turn them back and forth like he was turning a key in an ignition. This was considered repetitive behavior. He also exhibited an abnormal response to sensory stimuli (which he demonstrated initially within the first few weeks after he was born. He also spoke loudly, all of the time, even in places that needed softer voices, like church. He had an exaggerated emotional response and difficulty transitioning from one environment or setting to another.

Cody had obsessions as well, even as young as two years old. He was obsessed with the movie *Castaway*. He watched it at least 100 times over and would repeat the words from the movie. He repeated the name of the ball, *Wilson*, over and over. He obsessed over making origami, solving the rubix cube, computer games such as Minecraft, computers in general, then eventually music and electronic dance music (EDM), when he eventually became a DJ. When Cody became obsessed with something, it was all he talked about. He became an expert in each obsession and would use the internet to learn everything he could about a topic. When he told me or someone else about his obsession his eyes would light up, his smile became larger than life, and he would jump up and down with excitement.

At 16, Cody built his own personal gaming computer from scratch, ordering all the parts on the internet. He was well-versed in all the computer technology and how each part worked and what it did. His all-consuming obsessions caused him to have difficulty making friends. Unless the other child was into the same thing Cody was, they could not connect. It was difficult to find anybody who could relate to him.

In some aspects Cody was above average intellectually, but people with PDD/ASD do not learn the same way others do. In middle school, due to his emotional and behavioral issues, Cody was placed on an Individualized Education Program (IEP) in school that gave him a Behavior Aid who was always with him and would intervene when necessary. This was the only solution offered to address Cody's issues. So not only was Cody unique in his behaviors and thought patterns, now he also stood out even more because he had an adult accompany him throughout the day.

I felt so confused and helpless about how to help my son. The road was long and lonely. All that we were dealing with increased my depression, and the tension grew in my marriage. We rarely agreed on how to handle this situation with Cody. With three children and the challenges of Cody, there was no time or energy to put towards our marriage. My depression became so severe I withdrew, and I began to feel that our marriage was over.

We decided to go to marriage counseling. The therapist met with us a few times then requested to see me one-on-one. She came right out and asked me, "Do you want to be in this marriage?"

I thought about it and my answer was, "No." I felt so numb and had no love for him. I can't place all the blame on the struggles with Cody. Thinking back, I should not have converted to Mormonism or married him. I had a fairytale view and hope for what I thought a marriage should be without truly knowing myself or what I stood for. I adapted who I was for what I thought my husband wanted without being true to myself. I was a people pleaser, and this led to me feeling like I had lost myself within marriage and motherhood.

The therapist asked, "So then why are you still with him?"

I knew it was time for me to leave this marriage, but that thought made me physically ill. For some reason, I feared my husband (not physically but more mentally), and I feared confrontation in general. I had no clue

CHAPTER 3

what I was going to do or how I was going to do it. I put no thought into that. I just knew for my mental as well as overall health, it was time for me to start taking care of myself and find out who Diana was: mind, body, and soul.

CHAPTER 4
FIGURING IT OUT

December 27, 2004
Las Vegas, Nevada

I left the marriage counselor in a daze knowing what had to be done. I could not bear to continue in a marriage where I was miserable. I walked into our house and my husband was sitting on the couch.

I sat down next to him and he asked, "How was counseling?"

I replied, "Do you really want to know?"

"Yes, of course," he responded.

I could not believe the words that came out of my mouth as I spoke them, "I am leaving you." I was having an out of body experience. I was not consciously aware of what I was doing or what I was saying.

All he responded with was, "Get out." I walked up the stairs, went into my closet, and packed my clothes. While I was packing, my children followed me into the closet. I kissed them as I cried.

I don't know how I thought it was okay for me to leave the house and the children; but I was so desperate to find happiness, and myself, that I was willing to leave all that I had. I had nowhere to go but figured I could show up at my older sister's house.

I stayed there for a few weeks while I gathered my thoughts and made a plan. I laid in bed that night sobbing uncontrollably repeating, "I just want my children; I just want my kids."

I found a house to rent (from a friend to whom I had sold a new home). He had bought several investment homes that he then rented out. I had nothing – only my clothes. My head was spinning. I did not know where to begin. Luckily, we had just sold a house before moving into this current one and had made quite a profit. So I went and bought all new furniture and necessities for my own home.

Richard was quite angry. My leaving had taken him by surprise. Thankfully, we settled out of court, splitting everything in half, and we shared custody of the children. I never wanted to hurt him or take anything from him, especially not his children. He was a great father, but unfortunately, our relationship was neglected. And, in fact, we lacked compatibility from the beginning.

I do not blame him for the failure of the marriage. I did not know myself or what I wanted when I married him. Then Cody came along and the challenges we had with him put a strain on the marriage. Cody demanded a lot of attention and energy, and other things were pushed to the side. My postpartum depression played a role as well.

Sharing custody of the children meant they would spend time each week with me and also with their father. Going back and forth was not good for a child who had trouble with transition. Looking back, this was probably one of the worst things to put a child with Asperger's through. Packing a bag and dropping him off at school, only to be picked up and brought to another home with different rules and routines, was disastrous to Cody's mental health – and in the long run, probably for all of the children.

Savannah was just under 2 years old, Jessica was 4 and Cody was 5. So a routine was essential to keep things under control. I had a good routine as a single mother and my work schedule was pretty stable. I would get up at the same time every day and attempt to do the same things daily, which helped keep me grounded as well.

Cody's meltdowns and fits continued, maybe even worsened; but at this point it was just part of our lives. Many nights I would go to bed drained mentally and cry, wondering what I could do to help add peace to our lives and to help my boy. I still had no answers. The doctors, psychiatrists, and educators had no answers for me. I felt so alone. At some point I accepted that this was my life, and I had to make the best of it. Oddly, I never gave up hope that someday someone would offer an answer, or that Cody would miraculously have something click and he could live like most other people. This never happened.

Shortly after the divorce, the real estate market crashed. My job selling new homes for a builder in Las Vegas had been extremely lucrative. But when the market crashed, my income, based solely on commission, went to zero. I had bought a house by then and drove an expensive car, which was all within my means at the time. Since we shared custody, I did not receive any child support. And now I had no income. I emptied my 401K retirement account, hoping it was a temporary lull in the market. Nobody could have predicted how terrible the recession would be.

My home value dropped by $100,000 and after exhausting all of my savings, I had to do a short sale on my home and take a loss. Not quite as bad as a foreclosure, but definitely not great. I also had my car repossessed and thankfully bought an old car from Richard for almost nothing so at least I had a vehicle. I moved, yet again, into another rental home. All these moves were taking a toll on the children and on me mentally and physically. My stress level was high, and a child who was sensitive to his environment could feel the anxiety and stress.

When Cody was about 6 years old he became increasingly physically violent with his sisters and I was continually breaking up fights. I attempted to date, but introducing Cody to anybody was always stressful. Even girlfriends who had children judged his behavior, so I was reluctant to go anywhere or do anything when I had the children. Instead, I waited until they were with their father to see friends or go on dates. I became pretty serious with one man; but Cody's behavior stressed and worried me, so I decided it was not worth it.

Eventually I was in a serious relationship with a chiropractor who lived in Denver, CO. He was from Las Vegas and most of his family still lived there. He had one son who was 5. He handled Cody pretty well but there were numerous times when Cody was violent. One time he was acting out and my boyfriend spanked him. This caused a huge fight with Richard, who demanded nobody ever touch his son. I understood his concern, but I also knew how out of control Cody could be. I knew my boyfriend would never deliberately hurt my children and would only do this if it was 100% necessary. But I told him not to touch my children and to let me handle it in the future.

Co-parenting was extremely difficult, especially with Cody. He was still removed from class for disrupting or hurting other students. In elementary school, he had not yet been placed on an individualized education program (IEP) or had a Behavior Aide with him. The principal called multiple times, and Richard and I had to go down to the school to discuss Cody's behaviors. It was so embarrassing when we received a call from the school. I felt like a bad parent who could not control or discipline her child. We tried time-outs, verbalizing, and talking things out with Cody, as well as spankings. None of this worked. I had two other children for whom all these traditional ways of disciplining worked well. My daughters did not act like this – so what was I doing wrong?

At the same time, my professional life was a challenge. I tried to find jobs outside of real estate, but all the businesses in Las Vegas were hurting. Finding a job was very difficult and I gave up trying to make the kind of money I had made. I started thinking of leaving Las Vegas and moving to Utah, where Richard was from. We had spent a lot of time there, and had even had a vacation home there. Many of my children's relatives lived there. I looked online and applied for a job selling manufactured homes. I immediately received a call to interview and was hired on the spot! I loaded up my belongings and moved to Cedar City, Utah, about 2.5 hours north of Las Vegas, Nevada. I had discussed the move with Richard and he was supportive as he had grown up there: his family was there and ultimately he wanted to move back there as well.

CELEBRATING CODY

Memories of the Elementary School Afterschool Program

Jessica

Mr. Jordan, the After School Program Director, was so good for Cody. At our after school program, Mr. Jordan would drive some of us to the park or aquatic center. We were always the last to go because Cody was usually misbehaving. But Mr. Jordan was always so kind and understanding. He would jam out with us and play rock music and Cody would just laugh his head off. When Cody was happy his smile was larger than life and you could not help but smile too.

One time we were all outside flying kites and Cody was frustrated and attacking some of the other children. Mr. Jordan stepped in and Cody started going wild and getting violent towards him. Eventually, Mr. Jordan picked Cody up by his shoulders and sat him on a bench and held him there physically until Cody relaxed. Mr. Jordan was calmly talking to Cody. He was never mean to Cody. He always knew how to calm Cody down. Cody trusted Mr. Jordan.

CHAPTER 4

James Jordan

With Cody, it was a challenge to balance giving him room to grow and learn without compromising the classroom management. I quickly realized how creative he was. Whether it was origami, computers, or Rubik's cubes, Cody was always showing the class his discoveries and his talents. He loved to show his peers his origami designs and to teach them how to do them. Cody was so proud once the other students could do it themselves. I learned after much trial and error how to handle Cody when he was frustrated. I found that if I gave him a quiet space to do crafts, he would calm down and gain control of his emotions.

Cody was a leader in the class. He often organized skits or plays on the stage in the gym. But he was also very competitive in group games like dodge ball or hockey. I have to admit I loved how passionate he was and often held back my laughter when he'd trash talk the other team. Of course if he was called "out" he'd get pissed and trash talk opponents or teammates and it was not as funny.

CHAPTER 5
STARTING OVER

August 2006
Cedar City, Utah

I moved to Utah with $100 cash and my belongings. Thankfully, my older sister let me stay at her cabin just outside of Cedar City until I could find something permanent. The cabin was out west of town in a rural area, surrounded by trees and sagebrush. It was a true log cabin, two story, three bedroom, two bath, and it was on well water so the water was brownish and had a sulfur smell. But, I was grateful for a safe, clean place to live. Richard came up on the weekends and spent time with the children until he could permanently move up there himself.

My new job was a 20 minute drive into town and I was to start right away. Richard knew a family in Cedar

City that could watch Cody, Jessica and Savannah until school started. Many of the residents of southern Utah are Mormon and family is one of the highest priorities. My new boss must have noticed my financial struggles and gave me a $1200 bonus check, even though I had not sold anything yet. This extra money was a life saver, as I wasn't sure how I was supposed to buy food or put gas in my car until my first paycheck.

Someone also recommended I go on welfare, which I had not thought of since I have never been in such a terrible financial situation. I grew up middle or upper-middle class. We lived comfortably and I never really went without. That's not to say my parents did not go through hard times, but my father always worked, and my mother worked outside the home for most of my childhood. I showed up to the welfare office knowing nothing. The woman who helped me saw my confused look and realized I was not the typical welfare recipient. She helped me navigate the system, and I received a one-time payout, as well as food stamps, along with Medicaid health insurance for the children and myself. The one-time payout helped me secure a three-bedroom duplex that I moved into a couple of weeks later.

School started, and since I worked until 5:00 pm, the kids went to a daycare program after school. Savannah was in kindergarten, Jessica was in second grade and Cody was in third grade. I was anxious about how Cody would navigate the transitions from school, to a bus, then to daycare. One day I received a call from the daycare that the bus driver had to stop the bus because of Cody's behavior. The daycare informed me that they were not going to allow him to be transported on the bus if this continued. I had to find another means of care for my kids after school.

I discovered that the Red Rock Kids Club met right at the school and was run by the owner. It was less expensive and was onsite! I signed up all three children and hoped that Cody would not cause any problems. If this program did not work, there were no other options. Thankfully, the program was amazing. The students did crafts, created unique art, played indoor "hockey", and did homework. The owner did not seem to be phased by Cody's antics. This program was a life saver for me – one saving grace during such a stressful time.

While sitting in the cabin one night watching television, I saw an advertisement for nursing school, and felt an urge to go back to school. I had never really attended college more than one semester at age 19, and I failed one out of the two classes I took, and never went back. I felt the need to help people and make a difference – so nursing seemed to fit that description. At work, I met a girl who attended Southern Utah University. The owners allowed her to leave work to go to classes and were extremely flexible with her schedule. I looked into it further, went down to the financial aid office, and applied to enter into a four-year degree program. I would be considered a non-traditional student, due to my age and having children. I took a full schedule (four classes) and started out with general education such as English, Mathematics, and History. One year into my bachelor's degree I took Psychology 101 and found my passion for the study of the brain and behavior. It was then that I switched my major from nursing to psychology.

Fast forward three years to Middle School. It was no different from any other year for Cody: it was a challenge, but it did have some bright spots. Canyon View middle school in Cedar City, Utah, was a fairly small school and Cody's transition was helped because many of the same children from elementary school were in the middle school. But switching classes each hour proved too difficult for Cody, as transitions were always an issue for him, and for anyone with PDD or who is on the autism spectrum.

Fortunately Cody had a good friend, Brian, whom he met in middle school. Both shared similar interests, yet two friends were visibly so different. Brian had brown skin, dark hair and dark eyes. Cody was pale skin, blonde hair and blue eyes – but they loved hanging out. They both enjoyed magic and would make videos doing magic tricks. Cody watched endless videos on how to do the tricks. He became obsessed with Criss Angel, a famous magician and illusionist. I took Cody to a show in Las Vegas to see Criss Angel perform and he was elated. Magic was one of his obsessions; and while he was performing he would smile from one ear to the other; and I would savor those moments of happiness for my boy that seemed so overshadowed with more moments of misery. Brian was patient with Cody.

One night Brian slept over and the boys were making videos of tricks when they had an argument. I came out of my bedroom and saw Brian sleeping in the hall with a blanket and pillow. This was a pattern with Cody's relationships. He was rigid in his beliefs – if he felt he was right in any given situation, it would end in a negative manner. Brian was one friend that would forgive Cody, and they remained friends well into adulthood.

Cody and Brian also got into some trouble. In their creativity they made some fake *coins* that they would put into an office machine to purchase pens. This *coin* was made out of cardboard with a string attached, which tricked the machine into dispensing a pen. Essentially this was stealing, and law enforcement became involved. I was embarrassed and afraid that Brian's parents would blame my son and forbid Brian to hang out with Cody anymore. Things like this had happened in the past where Cody's behavior caused parents to stop letting their children spend time with him. I did not blame them, but it broke my heart as a mother.

In this case, no formal charges were placed; but we did have to go down to speak with a probation officer. This was Cody's first offense and the officer could see that we, as parents, were involved. He left the discipline up to us. I do not condone stealing, but I was impressed at Cody's creativity to think up such an elaborate scheme at 12 years old. It was both brilliant and scary.

This was how his brain worked: it was *constantly* thinking, and sometimes this led to bad things. If only I could have helped him channel this brilliance into something productive that would contribute to society! I feared his future could be filled with criminality and devastation. His intelligence was beyond anything I ever imagined, but too often it caused heartache and frustration. I tried to encourage him to use it to his benefit, and channel it into something that would be good for him. I dreamed that he could be a computer programmer like my father, who was a systems analyst for the government. Maybe Cody's natural abilities to understand computers could take him far if he could just focus.

CHAPTER 5

In his early teens, Cody loved to go deer hunting with his father. Hunting season in southern Utah was a huge thing – schools even closed for Fall Break. To preserve the wildlife, the number of deer that could be hunted was limited, and you had to submit your name to a pool. Deer hunting was a great bonding experience for Cody and his father. By this time Richard had moved back full time to Utah. They would go out early in the morning and walk miles in the forest, then go back out until dusk.

One year, Cody actually shot his own buck. Although Cody appeared tough, he was a very sensitive boy. When he shot the deer, they had to track it as it ran off until it died. Cody cried so much when he found the deer dead. Of course, this was not how you were supposed to act according to the other men and boys in southern Utah. Cody never really fit in with that crowd. He loved the mountains and nature; but he just did not fit into the hunting culture, or anywhere else either.

Cody struggled to fit in with any crowd. He would come to me crying that he did not understand where his place was. I loved his uniqueness, but as a growing teen I cannot imagine how this affected his emotional development. As human beings, we *need* to find our place in society, whatever and wherever that may be. I don't like cliques myself; but naturally, to make sense of our world, we must find categories and compartments. Belonging helps us. I wanted Cody to find that place in his world just so he felt some sort of acceptance and security.

CELEBRATING CODY
Memories from Brian

When I first met Cody, I thought he was the smartest kid because he was able to get all types of apps on his phone. He knew so much about technology and I couldn't even work his phone because all I had was a flip phone.

Cody was also really good at origami and made things for people at school.

Oh man, then we got really into magic! We would go to school and show everyone our magic tricks and they all loved it! Cody taught me this one trick: how to make a CD disappear in the newspaper. The CD was hidden with newspaper so the audience couldn't see it. The only problem was that we did the trick over top of the projector and did not realize that the light from the projector shone through the newspaper revealing the hidden CD. This is pretty funny, looking back. We may have been amateur magicians, but we did love it!

CHAPTER 5

We made videos of magic tricks to post onto YouTube. One of the videos had over 1,000 views! Sadly the YouTube channel got deleted though :/.

My biggest memory of Cody is when he and I made fake quarters out of cardboard to get candy out of quarter machines! We had sooo much candy we didn't even know what to do with it! We were rich!... with candy! We ended up getting in trouble for doing it – but I'm glad we did. It is one of the best memories I have of Cody.

CHAPTER 6
DANCING FOR HAPPINESS

July 2013
Las Vegas, Nevada

Once I graduated from Southern Utah University with my Bachelor of Science in Psychology, I moved back to Las Vegas, Nevada, where I had secured a job at a timeshare resort. Initially, I took Cody with me to live in Las Vegas since his dad had such a hard time with him. My daughters stayed with their father in Utah. This was extremely difficult for me to leave my daughters, but eventually, they would all move down to Las Vegas and live with me.

Cody's struggles followed him into his high school years. Cody was fixated on fairness in all and any situation in which he found himself. He could not overlook it when someone was not treated well –especially if he did not receive the same treatment as others. His high school, Spring Valley, was very large and located in Las Vegas, Nevada, with close to 2,500 students. This offered many opportunities for issues. I received multiple calls from the school because Cody had had an altercation with a fellow classmate or was yelling at a teacher. I became extremely acquainted with the dean of the school during Cody's 10th grade year. He was a no-nonsense kind of guy, big in stature with a mustache. He reminded me of a coach, which perhaps he used to be.

One call came from a riot-like situation in the courtyard. Cody loved to dance – and loved was an understatement. He took after me in this regard. Dancing is a sort of escape, and when he and I danced you could not wipe the smiles from our faces. He also loved electronic dance music (EDM), something he shared with his auntie Danielle, my twin sister. He taught himself to dance via YouTube videos. One of the popular dances in the EDM genre is shuffling. Cody would watch endless videos to learn how to shuffle and became very good at it. He and his aunt would practice together and he tried very hard to teach her – and many others – how to shuffle. He would do it no matter where he was, whether it be a grocery store or class.

CHAPTER 6

One day in the courtyard during lunch, he played music on his phone and was shuffling. Other students saw him and rushed over to cheer him on. When a crowd of students congregate, others rush over to see what they are watching. This caused hundreds of students to swarm around Cody, and they were getting loud, cheering him on. Cody struggled with fitting in and connecting with people, but when it came to music and dancing, it came naturally. The swarm of students naturally caused concern for the dean and teachers, as it is difficult to control a crowd of teenagers. I understood their concern; however, for once, Cody was not fighting or breaking any laws! He was doing something he loved and something others loved to watch.

The dean offered a compromise. He suggested Cody could perform at the next assembly, so at least it was in a controlled setting. Cody was ecstatic but also nervous. He began practicing right away and had a specific song and dance picked out: of course, EDM.

At the assembly Cody ran around the gym to each side where the students sat in the bleachers holding his hands up, which made the crowd excited, and all the students, approximately 2,500 of them, started screaming and yelling. The point of the song came to where he went and stood in the middle of the gym and when the beat hit, he started dancing. The crowd went WILD!! His euphoric smile was as large as the crowd. He put his heart and soul into it. Dancing and music is where Cody felt he belonged; it was where he connected to others. He finished his dance, and the entire gym screamed. My heart was full that my boy had made an entire school scream and cheer. Cody had this larger-than-life personality.

At the age of 16, Cody not only loved dancing, he also loved music. When he first heard Hardwell, a Dutch DJ and music producer, Cody fell in love with EDM. Hardwell became Cody's idol in the beginning, but there proved to be many more DJs Cody loved and followed. His dream was to be a #1 DJ. I knew if Cody was passionate about something, there was no half-assing it. I enrolled him in BLEND DJ school in Las Vegas. Lessons were one-on-one and cost $100 a session – not cheap. Anytime I had extra money, I signed him up for a class. The instructor said Cody had a natural knack for hearing the beats and timing of the music.

Cody went on to DJ friends' birthday parties and fundraisers. One of his best friends, Jessica, had a mother who did fundraisers, and she hired Cody to DJ for the annual walk. Cody was up all night creating a playlist of appropriate music. He was so nervous. Although he loved DJing, it was a bit limiting for him because he could not always play what he wanted; he had to play what others wanted. Cody also wanted to produce music. He went back to BLEND school to take production lessons and began to create his own music. Unfortunately, due to work and school, he did not have much time to devote to his passion. In his spare time he would mess around with music.

Cody kept getting kicked out of classes and suspended for disrupting classes, talking back to the teachers or fighting with other students. Academically, Cody always did well and he was very bright; but he was unable to learn in the standard school environment. So we pulled Cody out of the traditional school and enrolled him in an adult school, which allowed him to work at his own pace and graduate early. Even though the school was a long drive from our house and located in a bad part of town, it was worth it. The curriculum was self-paced, which gave Cody more freedom to learn how he wanted to learn. He was given packets of material that he read and worksheets he completed on his own, and there were teachers available to help guide and answer questions. This worked for Cody, because he despised being forced to do anything – so if he felt he was doing things of his own free will, he tended to go along with the idea. The more Cody was pushed, the more he fought back.

Cody graduated from high school in January of 2017, and went on to work at Krispy Kreme donuts as a cashier. Like most commitments in his life, this job did not last long.

CELEBRATING CODY

Memories from Dallas Lowry, Wrestling Coach

Cody was my favorite student – always kind and always smiling. His smile was one of a kind. Cody could tell when I was down and would always lift me up – he had a knack of lifting people's spirits. As long as you believed in him he was the best friend you could ask for. He would make class fun and entertaining, eventful and enthusiastic. He was the same in wrestling. He was very gifted in math.

One of my favorite memories of Cody was him sitting up on the mountain on a rock talking about life. He was full of love and kindness. My wife had just passed away and he had a way of letting me know everything was OK. Some days I would be hurting and there was his smile. I truly believe God blessed me with Cody Ward.

CHAPTER 7
CROSSFADED

May 2017
Las Vegas, Nevada

By now, Cody was an 18-year-old adult, but his moods and defiance continued. Most days he spent working, but was up all night in his room creating music. I suspected he was drinking because most of his friends did, but what happened next I could not have imagined.

I was at work when Jessica and Savannah – who were at home alone – called me.

"Mom! Cody is cross-faded and is asking to drink our pee!" Jessica said.

Wait, what?! Cody had come home from staying the night at a friend's house and apparently was intoxicated. It took me a minute to process what Jessica had just said. She proceeded to tell me that he first explained to Savannah that he has a fetish and that he liked to drink urine. My stomach dropped. *What the hell was going on? Am I in the twilight zone!?* The girls were so frightened, they had locked themselves in the bathroom, and he was knocking on the door begging them to please just pee in a cup so he could drink it.

Cody claimed he was high and drunk, which equals *cross-faded* in street slang. I was infuriated and scared all at the same time.

Savannah said that Cody walked in with a weird gait, then "went into his room, and then came back into the living room and asked me, *So do you know what a fetish is?*" Savannah replied, "Yes, why?"

Cody said, "My fetish is pee."

Savannah responded with, "Okay."

He asked, "Would you pee in a cup for me?"

Savannah said, "Eww, no, why?"

He responded, "That is my fetish and I want to drink it."

By then Jessica was awake and in the kitchen, and Savannah told Jessica what he said. Cody then came into the kitchen and proceeded to ask Jessica if she would pee in a cup for him.

Jessica replied, "No! If you want to drink pee, you pee in a cup!" Cody then peed in a cup and sipped his own urine.

The girls went into the bathroom and called Jessica's boyfriend and asked him to come over because they were scared. Cody went to his room and never came back out.

CHAPTER 7

The girls left with Jessica's boyfriend and then called me at work.

I called Cody and told him to pack his belongings and move out immediately. He denied everything; who knows if he even remembered doing it if he was high. He did pack his things; and by the time I arrived at home he was not there.

As a mother your job is to protect your child for 18 years, nurturing them, caring for them, guiding them, hopefully preventing them from getting hurt. Now I had to be the one to hurt my son and throw him out onto the streets to go slowly kill himself with drugs. My heart and mind screamed in agony. My heart broke. I began to fear for Cody's life. I saw the warning signs of the road he was headed down. The next two years would be a living nightmare. I found this excerpt on social media that resonated with me:

If you think quitting drugs is hard, you should try letting go of your child.

My Dear Child,

I feel like I'm saying goodbye to you and in a way, I suppose I am. I will always love you. I want the very best for you and I'm prepared to do the most unnatural thing a mother will ever do. My mind screams, I'm abandoning you.

Oh, I know you're all grown up, but to me, you'll always be my baby. Maybe that's part of the problem. My nature is to protect you. I see you broken and in despair – I'm broken and in despair too.

If you had cancer or heart disease, I would fight tooth and nail to get you the care you need. People tell me addiction is a disease and that you can free yourself anytime you want. Through abstinence and therapy, it seems so simple to me. You are dying. Please get help! But that's the thing about addiction, it's not simple – it's complex and thrives through denial and manipulation. It would be easier to stand at your hospital bed knowing I was helping you. But there is no hospital bed, there is no cancer or heart disease – only an insidious little secret – one that has grown into a horrific ugly beast. It is devouring you alive, and me along with it.

I've watched this monster grow. I pleaded with it, coddled it, and nurtured it. I've done everything I can to make this thing go away but it's relentless and I am left to face the truth. You my precious child are an addict. An addict. Oh my god, I loathe that word and yet it's true. Why does the truth have to be so hard? Even harder is what I still have to do.

CHAPTER 7

All my life I have watched over you and now I must set you free. Not because I want to, but because I need to. It is the only thing I can do that MIGHT save your life. But the process may also end it. There is nothing about this that feels good or loving, yet I am told by recovering addicts and other moms that have gone before me there is a greater chance you will succeed and get clean if I do this. Almost always letting go works. Believe me ALMOST is nowhere near comforting enough.

If I wasn't sure I was helping you to die by keeping you comfortable in your illness I would keep you clean by intervention, or growing weary of your consequences now that you are dealing with them, this insanity will stop.

If you think quitting drugs is hard, my dear, you should try walking away from your child. I know we both have grown sick from this monster, you are not the only one that needs help. I do too. I promise you I will do everything that is asked of me even if I think I am going to hate every minute of it. I'll do it because I know if I do, you might survive. I promise not to ask you to do anything I wouldn't do. I will ask you to take care but you will only smile and nod and carry on as before.

The words will only make me feel better; they are of no use to you at all. So instead, I shall give you to God; but before I do I will wrap you in your favorite baby blanket. The one you dragged behind you until it was nothing but rags. Lastly, I pray we both have the strength to do the next right thing, even when it feels so wrong.

I love you my precious child, may we both find peace forever and always,

MOM
-author unknown

There is no manual that is given to parents to know the right way to parent; but I knew that whatever we were doing now was not working. I would not allow my daughters to be subjected to his behaviors. But forcing Cody to move out was a ticket for him to do anything and everything he wanted, and that included drugs.

CHAPTER 7

CELEBRATING CODY

Memories from Jessica Smith, Best Friend

I first met Cody after his performance in front of the entire school. After watching him dance in front of hundreds of people, I knew there was something special about him. As soon as we met, we clicked.

Right when we became friends, he told me his dreams of being the number one DJ in the world. Right after he told me that, I set up my mom's DJ equipment and he DJ'd for a family party. Since then, for every event, I made sure Cody was living his dream, even if it was a small number of people he was the DJ for. We would pack up his car full of equipment and I would sit right next to him at his gigs, cheering him on as he was the #1 DJ in my eyes.

CHAPTER 8
HOPE AND DISAPPOINTMENT

January 2020
Las Vegas, Nevada

I was at work at a psychiatric hospital when I received a call from Cody. He said, "Mom, I'm going to die soon." It sounded ridiculous, but I believed him. He was sobbing. He said he had a vision that he would die soon – and I immediately started crying, telling him how much I loved him. At this time he was living in his own apartment, but we talked on the phone almost everyday. I felt a bit disconnected from him as he worked a lot. He came over sometimes, but not for very long. I was grateful just to see him.

Several days later he called me and said, "Mom, go look up at the sky, they're here, the aliens are here." It was early night time and I played along. I walked outside and looked up. My house was in a flight path for the international airport, so there were many lights in the sky from airplanes.

I replied, "Son, those are airplanes, not alien spaceships."

He was adamant and said, "No, mom, they are here, they are coming to help us. Don't be afraid of them."

Due to my education and working at a psychiatric hospital, I knew right away these were symptoms of psychosis. It is a mental disorder characterized by a disconnection from reality that usually presents with delusions, paranoia and hallucinations.

Several weeks passed and Cody called me again and said, "Mom, I'm at work and this customer teleported through the door to my work!"

I was now used to getting calls like this, and I found arguing with him or trying to convince him otherwise was pointless. In addition to my experience with my son, I also worked with psychotic patients in a psychiatric hospital. Someone with psychosis truly believes what they are thinking, hearing, and seeing, and only medications can pull them out of this state.

Things only became worse. Cody would call his father, his aunt, his sisters, or me in a panic, saying things like, "I am a shapeshifter… aliens are following me… I can talk to dogs and make them stay with my mind… I can control

CHAPTER 8

when doors open or street lights change… yucca trees are following me" (the latter from the movie *Rango*). The list goes on and on. We all reached a point we would just play along. It was not worth upsetting him.

Eventually, he became so psychotic that he stopped going to work, stopped eating, stopped drinking, and began driving randomly all around town. He would call us and say something really bizarre and then hang up. He was living in his own apartment at the time so we tried to keep tabs on him every day.

He would call and say, "I'm going out to Area 51 to find the aliens." And then he would hang up and not answer for hours. We were in fear of him actually driving out in his psychotic state and trying to enter Area 51 – and then getting shot by the military guards.

Cody ended up driving all around town, and called me to say, "I have to see Nicole (his ex-girlfriend at the time) to warn her."

Nicole was in cosmetology school, so I called the school and told them to call the police if Cody showed up there. I hoped that the police would put Cody on a Legal 2000 (an order to be admitted to a psychiatric facility). Instead, they just told the ex-girlfriend to go home for the day.

Cody arrived at the school only to find that Nicole had left. Cody then ran out of gas and had to hitch a ride with someone to Nicole's house. We asked Nicole to call the police in hopes of getting Cody help.

The whole family – Richard, his new wife, his sister, his best friend (both named Jessica), and I – drove over to Nicole's house. When we arrived the police were there speaking to Cody. We talked to the police who said that they had no grounds to arrest Cody. He was not suicidal nor was he homicidal. He was clearly delusional, but this was not considered criteria to place someone on a legal hold. We all knew it was time for him to go to a hospital to get help.

I even phoned the psychiatrist who worked at the hospital where I was employed. He spoke to the police, but had no luck in convincing them to hospitalize Cody. While we all were tip-toeing around with our words, and careful not to spook him, we were successful in persuading Cody to go to the hospital to talk to a doctor – just to make sure he was alright.

The psychiatrist that I worked for, who also was the hospital's medical director, had called ahead and told the emergency room to expect us. We arrived at the hospital where I worked and went into the emergency room. I explained the situation. It was a bittersweet moment. I felt some relief to know my son was safe, but sad that I had to hospitalize him against his will. I also knew, from my education and experience working in an inpatient psychiatric hospital, that the first psychotic break only means a lifetime of battles and struggles.

We left the hospital after they admitted Cody. The drive home was a long one. My heart broke once again, but I knew he would get the help he needed there.

While Cody was in the same hospital where I worked, I could not work on the unit he was in. I stayed on the geriatric unit on a different floor. The staff kept me informed that he was doing OK. One of my good friends was his psychiatric nurse, and she told me that he kept pushing the help button in his room, which triggered her to go check on him. He didn't really need anything; he just thought it was fun to push the button. She told me that he pointed out the window in his room and saw spaceships. "No they aren't; those are just airplanes, Cody." He made her laugh. She mentioned that his smile brightened up the darkness that filled a psychiatric hospital. She said he was a joy to treat.

It was a huge comfort having co-workers on the inside to let me know how he was doing and that they were taking good care of him. My heart breaks for family members who don't receive that type of communication. It is nerve-racking to not know how your family member is doing. I now take this compassion and empathy with me every day when I go to work in an inpatient psychiatric hospital. I know what it is like to be the person on the outside with a family member in the hospital. I strive every day to inform the family members and comfort them during their difficult times.

After five days, Cody was discharged from the hospital; he was still slightly delusional, but not as manic. His formal diagnosis was bipolar disorder with psychosis. We had moved him out of his apartment, knowing that he should not live alone or be in an environment that could trigger him to use drugs again. He had a history of drinking anything he could get his hands on as well as different hallucinogens – as far as I knew. But I was not aware of everything he used; and I did not know exactly when the drug use began, but I suspected it was around the age of sixteen. When we cleaned out his apartment, we found at least five large garbage bags full of empty cartridges of nitrous oxide (used for *huffing* or *whipitts*). We also found dozens of empty bottles of alcohol.

Strangely, his apartment was clean and tidy. That is one thing about Cody: he was oddly organized despite being psychotic. We stored all his belongings in my garage and he went to live temporarily with his father in Utah. That lasted only a week as he did not get along well with his stepmother. He had a delusion that she was trying to kill his father.

He then went to live with his grandparents in St. George, Utah. Again, that lasted only a week and then he came to live with me. I had the patience and knowledge of mental illness that enabled me to handle him and his psychotic behaviors probably better than anybody else.

Cody attempted to get jobs, but his mild psychosis and the medications he was on left him unable to learn a new skill; and he ended up quitting the job he had at the smoke shop. Slowly he returned back to himself and landed a job at Einstein's Bagels where he could walk to work. His car had been his father's, who took it back after Cody had abandoned it during his psychosis.

He eventually met a girl who he became pretty serious with. She was in the rave scene and he slowly entered back into that, which left me afraid that he would start using again. He also seemed to become more manic as time went on. I confronted him, asking if he was still on his medications. He lied and told me he was. He started spending a lot of time with his new girlfriend and his behaviors became more erratic and aggressive; he was arguing with me more and more.

I knew he had stopped taking his medications and started using drugs again. I confronted him and told him if he did not take his medications he could no longer live with me. He admitted he had stopped due to the sexual side effects.

After weeks of fighting and demanding he move out, he did. Another crack in my heart and soul. He had nowhere to live. He was homeless. He was living in his car. I begged and pleaded for him to just take his medications and stop using. He refused.

He said, "This is me, Mom. I use drugs, I am not going to stop; they help me."

I responded, "Help you? Help you? Are you kidding me, they are ruining your brain and your life!"

For the next few months, he slept in his car. He showered at a recreational center. He would visit the house from time to time and I would feed him. I continued to offer him a place to live as long as he quit using, but he would never agree to it. He delivered for DoorDash on the side for money, and hopped from one job to the other. At one point he was a car valet, but he came to work drunk one morning and was fired. He could not keep a job mostly due to his drug and alcohol use.

One person whom he turned to often was my identical twin, his auntie Danielle, who he nicknamed Schmant.

CHAPTER 8

She had a nickname for him too, Noodles. This came from a time when I would say, "He's my punkin' noodle pie." Cody and Danielle had a bond since day one like no other. They bonded over music and the rave scene. She was in the rave scene back in the 1990s and he was into the modern electronic music scene. They would video chat for hours talking about music and exchanging their likes and dislikes. He often said, "Danielle gets me." They were extremely close and would go to see one of her favorite DJs from the 1990s, Dieselboy. Cody fell in love with drum and bass, and the genre of electronic music. They would go to different drum and bass shows together. Danielle would check in on him, and let me know how he was doing because he would open up to her.

The next few months were another downward spiral for Cody, one I could not save him from. The boy we knew was slowly slipping away. I often wondered, *How am I supposed to live each day knowing my son is on the streets using and neglecting his mental and physical health*? This was not natural.

CELEBRATING CODY

Memories from Jessica

One night when I was having relationship issues with my boyfriend I asked Cody to come spend time with me because I was lonely and sad. He didn't hesitate and came right over.

We got into a deep conversation of life and the things we had been through growing up. I told Cody about a girl who had cerebral palsy and how so many people were mean to her and he started sobbing. I grabbed his hand and held it tight and told him that she was okay, she was so happy and positive and was living a great life despite her past.

He sobbed and said to me, "But how can people be so mean to a beautiful person?" I hugged him and let him know that he is such a sympathetic person – that's what makes him special because you don't come across such an empathetic person very often – especially a man.

CHAPTER 9
SEARCHING FOR CODY

Cody stopped by my house and appeared paranoid and distraught. It was at a time when Savannah was staying with me during summers, weekends and holidays, while she lived with her father when school was in session. Jessica lived with me full-time. Both girls were a great support for me during these hard times with Cody and his psychiatric challenges.

Cody was running around the house messing with different electrical items. I called his best friend, Jessica, and asked her to come over to see if she could talk him into going back to the hospital. When she did, he ignored her. He continued turning on and off appliances because he was paranoid that the government was spying on us through them. He even went upstairs and turned off all the breakers, which turned off all the lights and power.

I yelled, "CODY!" and he quickly turned them back on. He came downstairs, plugged his phone into a charger near the TV and went out the front door. We all looked at each other – puzzled. *Where is he going?* We thought he might have just stepped out front to get fresh air, but he did not come back inside. Jessica and Savannah followed him as he was walking to his car, and asked him to stop.

He pointed up to the sky and said, "That's Donald Trump flying into Las Vegas."

They asked, "Where are you going?"

He responded, "I have to get this thing off my car because the government is tracking me." He was messing with some strange black box that had a blinking red light on it that was attached to his driver's side mirror. His sisters talked him into coming back into the house; but he left again and did not return. Jessica was always there for me when I needed her to try to talk some sense into Cody. She left in disappointment; but I thanked her repeatedly.

It was late so I went to bed. Then a call came through from Cody's phone. *Where was he?* Savannah quickly answered it. "Hello?"

A man responded, "Hi, is this Ms. Ward?"

CHAPTER 9

Savannah replied, "This is Savannah Ward, who is this?"

This person on the other end of the phone handed the phone over to Cody who told us that he was driving out to the desert and his car ran out of gas. He had walked to this person's house to use the phone. I was furious and scared all at the same time. It was nighttime, and Cody was in another psychotic break, causing major chaos for my family again. *But what was I to do?* Ignoring it would not make it go away.

I got dressed and drove 45 minutes to the other side of town looking for Cody and his car. I found him standing in the middle of the road on a median and he was freezing. He then guided me to where his car was. He had left it outside the entrance to a very nice gated community.

I thought to myself, *Oh, I'm sure these residents love seeing this. Let's hope a towing company doesn't come to take it.* I drove Cody to the nearest store, purchased a gas can, drove to the nearest gas station and filled it up with gas. We then drove to his car, filled the gas tank, and he followed me home. All the while Savannah was lecturing Cody telling him, "When we get home you are giving me your keys and going to bed and you are not leaving, OK?"

Savannah is a natural at nurturing others. She handled Cody well – she knew what to say and how to say it so

Cody would listen. Growing up, those two fought like cats and dogs and seemed like oil and water. I think they are actually a lot alike, and that's why it was hard for them to get along when they were younger. But they loved each other dearly. I reluctantly let Cody stay because my rule was that he can only move back in if he stopped using drugs. But I figured for one night I would let it slide. He was safe, and I could get some sleep.

The next morning Cody was trying to leave. Savannah did not want him to but he promised he would be OK. A few nights passed and I was about to go to bed when a video chat came through from Cody. My stomach always dropped because I feared what I would find out if I answered his call.

I answered, "Hello?" A man's voice came through.

"Hi, is this Cody's mom?"

I said, "Yes."

He proceeded to inform me that I should probably come pick up Cody because he was in the middle of an intersection on top of his car blasting music. I replied, "No, I am not picking him up. He needs to go to a psychiatric hospital, so I suggest you call the police."

The man replied, "I already did and they will not do anything because he is not suicidal or homicidal."

I responded, "What the hell is wrong with these police? Clearly he is delusional and a danger to himself!"

CHAPTER 9

The gentleman on the other end agreed. So, once again, I dressed and headed to Cody. When Jessica and I pulled up, we saw his car pulled off to the side of the road. It was in pretty bad shape. He had removed the windshield wipers and the brakes were really bad – he had used the emergency brake to stop at lights (his delusions told him this was a good idea). This car was actually his father's and he was making payments to his dad to buy it.

Several men (a neighborhood security guard and another passerby) were standing around my son who was lying on the ground wrapped up in a blanket as it was winter and very cold. The gentleman who called me was John; he was headed to an evening job when he stumbled upon Cody.

He said, "You probably shouldn't go over to him because he is talking badly about you. I think you might be a trigger for him."

I kept my distance. We stood around discussing what our next steps should be. We decided I would drive Cody's car back to my house, and my daughter would drive my car with Cody in it.

Cody kept repeating, "You're evil." Strange, as I was the one who continually rescued him and bailed him out. I knew it was the psychosis talking and so I kept my distance and just went to bed. Jessica stayed with him for a bit downstairs and he eventually went to bed. He left the next morning once again – who knows where he went.

One week later I received a call from Desert Springs hospital where Cody was in the psychiatric hold unit under a Legal 2000. The police found him wandering around in a hotel lobby with one shoe on and talking nonsense. They asked if I would pick him up and I said *absolutely not* – he needed to stay in there and get some help. It was just a few days before his 21st birthday.

He was discharged from the hospital on his birthday, January 19, 2020. Once again, I allowed him to move back in with me, but this time I had drawn up a contract. He would need to sign it and agree to: stay on medications, see a therapist, get substance abuse treatment, and get a job within the next 30 days. He reluctantly signed it – after trying to negotiate.

He had a follow-up appointment with the state psychiatric provider and I drove him to it to ensure he went. During the drive, he was arguing with me about why he did not need to be on medications. He became irate and was pounding on the dashboard and screaming at me. I was very scared he might hit me. We arrived and sat down with the female psychiatrist who asked why he was there.

I explained a little but Cody interrupted and stated, "I don't know, but I am not taking any medications."

CHAPTER 9

He then started yelling at the psychiatrist. Other workers looked into her office to make sure everything was OK. Cody stood up and stormed out and left the appointment. I followed him and told him if he was not going to take medications then he could not live with me.

The next few months were tumultuous – full of fights and verbal abuse. I kept threatening to kick him out as he was not following any of the agreed upon points in the contract. After six months, Cody found his own apartment. He had kept a job for a few months as an Amazon delivery driver, and made decent money. He was approved for the apartment all by himself and I was pretty proud of him. He seemed to be somewhat sober, so my hopes were high for my boy. He and I moved him into his one bedroom apartment and once again, his best friend Jessica Smith brought over food and decorative items for his new home. Little did I know this would be his last.

CELEBRATING CODY

Memories from James Jordan, Afterschool Program Director

Cody felt everything so deeply for a kid. When he laughed he laughed loudly, he smiled wide, he was compassionate, loyal and loved deeply. His frustration, his pain and his anger he felt just as deeply. When his anger would get the better of him, it could last for hours. Cody was a complex kid who suffered mentally more than I can imagine. When Cody was frustrated and angry he was hard to be around, but when he was in a good place he was so giving, so funny, creative and loving.

CHAPTER 10
A MOTHER'S HOPE

As parents we tend to see all the potential our child has. In Cody I saw a genius – someone with a high IQ. His ability to learn new things blew me away. He was self-taught when it came to computers and DJing. He taught himself how to solve the rubix cube in less than a 1 minute. If he would have persevered with computers he could have worked for the government as a professional hacker. He could have been a world famous DJ. His energy and passion was wasted.

I do not know for sure what is to blame: drugs, mental illness or society. Blaming doesn't change anything anyway. My soul burned with such a desire and passion for him to follow his dreams. I wanted, more than anything, for him to succeed in life. He could have changed the world. I'm angry at him – angry at the mental health system – angry at the drugs – and angry at society for how they treated him at times.

How many other mothers or fathers out there watch their loved ones deteriorate right before their eyes due to addiction? What we are doing as a society in the United States is not working. Drug use costs the United States over $600 billion every year. In 2021, the National Institute of Mental Health reports one in five U.S. adults live with a mental illness – this means 57.8 million people.

Through my professional work, I have met many drug addicts. It is standard practice during admission to an inpatient psychiatric facility that a urinary drug toxicology screen is done. This helps the doctors and staff know how to treat the patient. Psychosis can be drug-induced, and that is important in diagnosing.

Cody tested negative for drugs most of the time due to his drugs of choice. One was ketamine, which has several other names: Special K, K, ket, kitkat, super k or horse trank. Some of the effects of ketamine use are: "feeling happy and relaxed, feeling detached from your body (falling into a k-hole), visual and auditory hallucinations, confusion and clumsiness, increased heart rate and higher blood pressure, slurred speech and blurred vision, anxiety, panic, violence and vomiting." (Alcohol and Drug Foundation of Australia.)

CHAPTER 10

Another drug Cody frequently used was nitrous oxide. This is typically used in cans for whipping cream. It is also used as laughing gas in dental offices. On the street, this drug is often referred to as *whippits*. My son purchased it at a smoke shop as a whipping cream dispensing unit. Breathing in the nitrous oxide from whipped cream chargers is a type of inhalant abuse, also sometimes referred to as huffing. The effects of huffing may include: "euphoria, lightheadedness, vitamin B12 deficiency, delusions and hallucinations, damage to peripheral nerves, muscle weakness, spinal cord disease, paralysis in the legs, brain damage and asphyxia." (bluffsrehab.com)

Another drug Cody used was DMT, or n-dimethyltryptamine, a naturally occurring chemical found in the brain as well as in plants (mainly indigenous to Central America). DMT is a hallucinogenic drug and can be snorted or smoked. The effects of DMT are: intense euphoria, hallucinations, and new perceptions of reality that people often characterize as life-changing. In addition, the user may experience dizziness, headache, heightened body temperature, increased heart rate, loss of muscle control, nausea and vomiting, and pain or tightness in the chest. (www.addictioncenter.com)

The reason Cody typically tested negative for drugs is because most tests do not test for these types of drugs. Not a lot is known about the long-term effects of these drugs due to their rarity. The other question that always lingered in my mind was, *Did the drugs cause the psychosis, or did he have a mental illness? Would he have had psychosis eventually without drug use? Or was his mental illness the underlying factor and the drugs triggered it?* It is hard to know for sure; but one thing is certain – *drugs and mental illness do not mix*. This did not stop Cody from using them, and unfortunately, they made his illness worse.

October 2020
Las Vegas, Nevada

Things with Cody continued to be a challenge. My twin sister Danielle came to visit us in Las Vegas from Florida, where she had moved. She was arriving late, so I allowed Cody to pick her up from the airport using my car. (His father had taken away the car he had let him drive after his last psychotic break.) On the drive from the airport, Danielle noticed that Cody was slurring his words and driving erratically – stopping at green lights and failing to stop at red lights. Danielle offered to drive, but Cody refused. He denied that he was drunk.

When my sister told me what happened, I went into my car and found a Gatorade bottle that reeked of vodka and what appeared to be vomit all over my middle console.

CHAPTER 10

When I confronted Cody he denied it all and we had a big argument. I insisted he move out, yet again.

This time, alone with no one looking over his shoulder, he had more opportunities to drink and use drugs.

One evening Cody called me to ask for advice: "Mom, do I stay at the scene if I hit someone (in his vehicle) after we exchange insurance information and nobody is hurt?" He added, "We've been waiting for the police to show up and it has been forever. I am doing doordash and this is cutting into my time to work and make money."

I responded with, "Well, as long as you exchanged insurance information and they are not injured I guess it is ok." Supposedly, as he side-swiped someone, it hit his passenger side mirror and broke it. The other car did not have much damage, according to Cody. I'll never really know if that is what truly happened. This car was one that he had bought off his friend who was a mechanic. This car was in great shape mechanically – a little beat up on the exterior, but reliable enough for him to do his doordash and drive to and from work.

According to Savannah, Cody drank every night until he passed out. Surprisingly, even during his extreme drug and alcohol use, he still worked. He often did doordash to earn extra money. He was extremely motivated by money, something he inherited from his father. Money never motivated me. I made sure I paid my bills but to me life was for enjoying, not working.

One morning at work, I received a missed call from a number I did not recognize. It went to voicemail, and it was Cody. "Hi mom, I just wanted you to know I am in jail. I was arrested last night for a DUI. I am getting out this morning, but the police took my phone, so I am walking to go buy a new one."

Later, Cody called Savannah, who was at school (she was a senior in high school). He apologized excessively, and was crying hysterically. Savannah fell to the ground sobbing, worried about her brother. We all worried about him and where he was headed so much, but none of us could stop him.

Cody was working as a delivery driver for Amazon; and knowing that he would eventually lose his driver's license because of the DUI, he quit to find a job where he did not have to drive. He found a job at BrightSolar, setting up appointments for people to have solar energy installed in their homes.

He found an attorney and fought to keep his driver's license. He wanted to have a breathalyzer machine put in his vehicle that would allow the car to start. This way, he could still drive to work. The fact that his car accident was minor and no one was severely injured was a godsend.

CHAPTER 10

So many lives are lost due to drunk driving; the fact that he was caught before more damage was done was a blessing.

Cody continued to drink heavily but not drive when he did, at least from what he said. Addicts lie and they lie *A LOT,* so I was always hesitant to believe anything he said. But Cody tended to speak his truth even if it hurt.

CELEBRATING CODY

Memories from James Jordan, Afterschool Program Director

Cody loved the idea of being in love. He ALWAYS talked about this girl or that girl and how hot they were. Some of the girls that he liked were girls in the club. One time he and a girl went onstage in the gym and kissed behind the curtains. Other girls were not as receptive to his affection. He had a hard time figuring out why they didn't like him in return, which usually led to him becoming angry.

CHAPTER 11
GRANDMA PENNY

Grandma Penny, Richard's mom, was Cody's protector. From day one, she stood between Cody and anyone who wanted to pick on him or cause him any grief. In 2020, Penny was diagnosed with pancreatic cancer and the news shocked us all.

Penny was the glue that held the family together. She was the first to plan holiday gatherings and cook the most amazing dishes. She was known for her selflessness. She loved her children, but seemed to love her grandchildren even more. Throughout Cody's drug use, he distanced himself from family, and especially from Penny, knowing well what she would say about his life and how he should change.

The knowledge of her cancer diagnosis hit my children hard, but Cody had a strange response: he did not want to go visit her. "That's not how I want to remember her; and if it's her time to go, then it's her time to go."

I thought he would want to be the first one to spend time with her, but he did not – again, probably due to drug use. Eventually we convinced him to go visit with her and he did. They went fishing; and the picture of Cody and his grandma at the lake smiling the biggest smiles is a family treasure! My daughter put that photo in the middle of a huge collage with dozens of pictures of Cody. The feeling of love and contentment shines through that picture.

The months passed and Grandma Penny became weaker. Chemotherapy caused her to lose weight and her hair. Penny was a hairstylist, so her hair had always been perfect. The loss of her hair was devastating. The family felt she would go before Christmas – her strength was fading quickly. She passed away peacefully on Christmas Day, 2020, at her home in St. George, Utah, surrounded by her husband and children. The news hit my children extremely hard.

Jessica and Savannah planned to go to the funeral, but hesitated to invite Cody because of his drug use and bizarre behavior. I insisted that he needed to go – she was his grandma, too. The girls reluctantly offered to drive up with him. They tried so hard to keep their distance when he was like this, and now they had to spend three hours in a car ride with him. They were not looking forward to it.

They arrived in Utah at their father's house. The mood was sorrowful and they talked and reminisced about their grandma. If you disagreed with Cody or accused him of being wrong about something, he could go from 0-60 in two seconds; there was no talking him down when he reached this point. Jessica and Savannah were discussing what they might read or get up and say at the funeral, and kept asking their father for his input. Something about that triggered Cody's anger, and he began yelling at them.

Cody yelled, "Shut up. You already asked and we told you what you should say. Stop repeating yourself."

This type of thing would not trigger a *normal* person and seemed so minor and irrelevant. But with mental illness, addiction, high emotions and sensory overload, Cody could go into a complete rage.

Their father chimed in, trying to defuse the situation; unfortunately it made things worse and then their father became the target of Cody's fury. When Cody became angry, he pulled out his arsenal of bad memories and thoughts, and verbally attacked with razor sharp words – words that he knew would dig deep and hurt. In the mental health field, we refer to this as *hurt people, hurt people.* In essence, when someone is hurting, they turn that pain towards others and try to hurt them as much as they are hurting.

When it escalated to the physical, their father told him to leave. So Cody said he was going home and would not attend the funeral. Their Dad begged him to just cool off for the night, and please stay to attend the funeral. As the stubborn person that he was, Cody refused. He got in the car to drive back to Las Vegas, and called me, sobbing.

As I picked up the phone, I thought he was crying due to his grandma's death. He told me that he was driving back and not staying for the funeral. He then said that he did not want to stay on this earth any longer and that he just couldn't take it.

I begged and pleaded that he stay and go to his grandma's funeral, but he would not change his mind. I then attempted to talk him out of taking his own life, as I had done numerous times before. I could usually talk him out of it quickly, and typically did not panic too much when he made these statements. But this time, knowing the devastation of losing his grandma, I was frightened that he might just do it.

I hung up with him and then called my daughter to find out what really happened. As usual, Cody's version of events was skewed to his advantage.

CHAPTER 11

While I was on the phone with his sisters, Cody called my twin sister and said, "I can't do this life anymore. I am up in the mountains and I'm done. I am going to end my life." Thankfully, she talked him out of it, and he went home.

CHAPTER 12
LETTING GO

2021, Florida

It was time for a change. My children were grown: Savannah was about to graduate from high school; Jessie (Jessica) was 21 years old; and Cody was living out on his own at age 22. My sisters, Denise and Danielle, had moved out to a small beach town in Florida, and asked me to move there too. I always wanted to make my way back to the beach. I was afraid to leave my children and be so far from them, but California was too expensive. This was my time now, so I decided to move to Florida. In the middle of January, I loaded up my car to make a three-and-a-half-day drive to Florida by myself.

The night before I left, I had Cody come over to give him a few things and say goodbye. There were no tears: in fact, I tried to hurry him off as I saw him getting agitated. Many of our encounters were like that. I would see his mood become unstable and his irritability increase, and I would leave, or end the visit to avoid a blowout. This weighs heavily on my heart. I know it wasn't ill intended; it was my way of surviving, mentally and emotionally. His energy was always so intense that most days I just couldn't handle it.

He ended up going through the garbage that I put out on the street and took many food items and other things. He was mad at me for not offering them to him. I hugged him and told him I loved him so much. And that was it. Little did I know this would be the last time I would see or feel my boy.

I left the next morning to take Savannah to Utah to finish out her Senior year of high school; then I made the trek to Florida with my dog Otis. I was a nervous wreck. I am a pretty independent woman, but driving across the country alone for 10 hours a day was nerve-racking. I had a brand new car, but there was always the chance of a blown tire, or something else going wrong. It was also winter, so I was nervous about snow storms. Luckily, the weather was pretty good the whole way. I did not sleep well during those nights on the road, and was very anxious the whole time. I will never do that again.

CHAPTER 12

I arrived in Florida on February 1, 2021. Within 30 days I had secured a job as a therapist at an inpatient psychiatric hospital.

One day I was sitting at my desk at work, and my heart sank. I was scrolling through my phone looking at pictures and memories of Cody. It had been two months since we had talked. I had sent him a couple messages such as, "I love you son, I miss you, hope you are well." But he did not respond.

I even tried to send him an email apologizing for our last interaction. I had blocked him because of something that was very disturbing to me. Cody had told Savannah that he had a sexual dream about her. It made Savannah feel uncomfortable and so she had shared that with her father. I was so fed up with these weird thoughts, obsessions, and behaviors from Cody that I blew up! I was frustrated with how his drug use and lack of treatment for his mental illness had caused so much heartache to the family, especially my daughters. I was done! I texted him telling him to never talk to his sisters again and get some help.

He defended himself saying, "It was only a dream. I was just sharing it with her to let her know that dreams have messages." He went on to say, "This family is so closed off to sexuality and we need to be more open about it."

I was so tired of it all I blocked him. Two months later, sitting in Florida, I felt guilty. I had shut out my son and never really gave him a chance to explain. I missed him terribly. I had my sisters reach out to him in hopes he hadn't blocked them and would respond. My oldest sister, Denise, received a short text back saying, "I'm good, Aunt. I miss you and love you." But nothing more.

This was good news – he was still alive and seemed OK. My twin sister reached out to him through a texting app, and he responded with anger saying he didn't want anything to do with her since she had sided with me. It was hurtful. I worried about Cody not having contact with his aunt, who had always been by his side. Danielle and I were the two that understood him and tried to love him unconditionally. *What would happen to him with no support system?* I knew that was a recipe for disaster.

A few weeks later, I sat at my desk, and I started crying uncontrollably. My heart worried for my son like never before. I felt something bad had happened to him but I could not contact him. These next few days were filled with anxiety. I was shaky, and my mind was racing. I felt scared but could not put my finger on why. My work suffered, and I could not focus. It was hard for me to hold groups for my patients. On my lunch breaks I would sit in my car and do tapping techniques to try to calm my

CHAPTER 12

anxiety. *What is going on with me? I haven't felt like this in years. Could it be a mother's intuition of what was to come?*

Looking back, that's exactly what it was.

A few days later, on Tuesday, April 27, 2021, I was in the outside atrium at the psychiatric hospital working with a group. My phone started buzzing and it was *Cody*! My son was calling! It had been almost three months since I had talked to him. I thought to myself, *Do I answer? Do I want the drama that might unfold*? I grabbed the phone and answered, "Hello?"

The familiar voice of my son: "Hi Mom."

I replied, "Hi dude."

He said, "How are you?" I said, "I'm good, how are you?"

He responded with, "Not good Mom. Someone is planting microscopic drugs in my house, at my job, everywhere, and I don't know what to do."

I thought to myself *he's delusional. He's paranoid. Here we go again.* My heart and soul could not take another psychotic break, especially with me so far away.

I tried to console him and went along with the delusion, "Well, you should call the police and have them find out who is doing this." In the back of my mind, I thought if the police were involved, they would see that he was not mentally well and they would get him the help he needed. But thinking back to the other times I called the police, my hope dwindled, knowing they probably wouldn't help him – because "he is not a danger to himself or others."

Cody started crying. "I'm lost mom. I don't know what to do."

I said, "I'm sorry, son, I love you."

He stopped crying and asked sincerely, "How are you doing out in Florida, Mom? Are you OK?"

I said, "Yes, son, I'm OK. I actually really like it out here. I'm at work now."

He responded with, "Oh, that's good, Mom. I'm so glad."

I told him I had to go since I was at work and we ended the call. That was the last time I would hear my son's voice. Little did I know what was to unfold only a few days later.

I woke up the next morning to a few missed calls from Cody at around 11:00 pm my time. I turn off my phone at night. He didn't leave a message or text. I sent him a text that I still have stored in my phone.

"Hey dude I just woke up and saw I missed your call. I was sleeping, hope you're OK luv u."

CHAPTER 12

No response. A few hours later I tried calling his phone, but it went straight to voicemail. The next day I called again – voicemail. The next few days I kept calling.

There was still no answer.

CHAPTER 13
THE LONGEST FLIGHT

May 1, 2021, 8:06 p.m.
Ft. Myers, Florida

The voicemail I heard that day would forever change my life. "Hello, this is Officer John Wilson with the Las Vegas Metro Police Department. I am hoping you can help me, please give me a call at…."

Listening to the voicemail, I instantly thought, *oh no, what did Cody do now*? I had so many memories of different incidents involving Cody and the police that part of me was no longer shocked when I received a call from law enforcement. There was the time he was found on top of his car in the middle of the intersection. Another time was when he was admitted into the psychiatric hospital after being found without one shoe on, wandering through a hotel lobby.

This time was different. This would be the last call I would ever receive regarding my son.

I called the officer back immediately. This is where the nightmare begins – the nightmare that no mother wants to endure.

"Officer Wilson, hi, I just missed a call from you, this is Diana Ward."

"Yes, are you the mother of Cody Ward?"

Reluctantly I answered, "Yes." The Mount Charleston Police had found his car that had been parked up in the mountains for a few days, and they were wondering if I knew anything about it. I didn't.

My mind started racing. I knew he went up there a lot and I knew he did a lot of drugs. My worst fear – he had overdosed on ketamine. I informed the officer of my son's history with mental illness and drug abuse. He assured me they would keep looking for him and, if need be, file a missing person's report. Officer Wilson said to give him a few hours to work on this case and he would call me back.

My thoughts returned to the many times my son said, "I don't belong on this earth, I don't fit in, I want to leave this earth." The many times my heart ached for my son and I hoped I could just *will* him to happiness. The countless nights I lay in bed sobbing, not knowing how to help

CHAPTER 13

my son, who since the day he was born, seemed to struggle in his own mind and body.

Minutes passed that felt like hours; hours felt like days. My daughter and I called the officer back at least 15 times, with no answer or return call. I lay in my bed in a fetal position crying, "I just want to hold my boy."

My heart knew. My soul knew what was coming.

The phone rang. I answered, and a woman's voice said, "Is this the mother of Cody Ward?"

I respond, "Yes."

"Unfortunately, I am calling from the Clark County Coroner's office."

Silence. I leave my body and hear nothing. I drop the phone. My daughter raised the phone up to her ear, listening. She screams, "NO, NO, NO, NO, NO!!" This is the beginning of the end of all that I knew.

This is the point in time that we forever mark as ACD (after Cody died).

After receiving the call from the coroner, I paced back and forth from room to room, repeating in my mind, *I need to get to Vegas. I need to get to Vegas.* My heart longed to be back to where my son's last days were. I'm not sure why or what I thought that would accomplish. I grabbed some of my belongings and threw them in a suitcase while my sisters figured out flights. I had hung up on the coroner's office but they had information to give me.

My phone rang. I answered, "Hello?"

The lady on the other line said, "I have some important information to give you in regards to your son's belongings."

I thought, *I don't give a fuck what you have to say to me or what information you have! I cannot process this right now!* She rambled on and I wrote down a case number and where they were taking his body. I had to go into my bathroom and shut the door because I could not hear her over my twin and daughter crying and screaming. *Why did I have to be the one to be the secretary during this time? This was MY son!?*

It's strange what the brain can do during times of crisis. Now I can compartmentalize during times of crisis, which allows me to complete extremely difficult tasks. However, my meltdown tends to come later.

In between the calls from the coroner, Richard was calling, sobbing. His heart was still trying to heal from the loss of his mother.

Denise was trying to book flights – her husband, Tom, had to take over since she was a mess. He booked the wrong date. Eventually we purchased flights and our friend drove us to the airport. By this time, it was 1 a.m. and we were all still sobbing, but a little less frantic.

My fight or flight response had kicked in and I had diarrhea. I kept having to go to the bathroom. There was nobody in the airport and it was dark. We sat crying and looking through our phones at pictures of Cody for six hours until our flight left.

We were trying to get a hold of Jessica, who had gone camping out in the desert in Las Vegas, and had no cell phone service. I had called her boyfriend's parents and asked them if they could get a hold of their son and they said they tried with no luck. My panic came and went in waves. I just needed my other daughter near me – having my children near me always grounded me; now, I would never have one of my children near me again.

We finally boarded the plane to Las Vegas, with intermittent bouts of sobbing. By this time we had been awake for over 24 hours and I felt like a zombie. I was having an out of body experience. The flight attendants keep telling us to keep our masks on due to Covid-19. This was tough as we kept blowing our noses.

The flight attendants would ask, "Are you ok?"

I thought, *NO! Fuck no, we are not OK!*

I responded softly and just said, "My son just passed away."

The flight attendant brought back bottles of water for us. I wanted to scream "Do you think this bottle of water is going to help bring my son back!!??" But I know they were just trying to do something to help us feel a little better.

While sitting in the airport during a layover, we finally reached my parents. With the three hour time difference, they had still been sleeping and had not heard the news. I called and my Dad answered. I cried into the phone, "Daddy, Cody's dead. They found his body in the mountains."

He responded, "Oh no, honey, that's terrible. I'm so sorry."

My father was stoic but I heard a tremble in his voice. I think I got my ability to cope during an extreme crisis from him. He does not cry often, nor do I. It's not that we are unfeeling, but we tend to cry in private.

We finally landed in Las Vegas, and my father picked us up from the airport. I do not recall getting off the plane or walking out to the parking garage. I just remember running to my Dad with my twin, and him holding us as we sobbed. By this time, Jessica had received the news. She met us at my parents' home along with my niece, Brittanee. As we pulled up to their house, my daughter and my niece met us in the garage. I ran to my daughter – I had to have her in my arms to make sure she was OK. We held each other and sobbed.

My mother made us lunch, but of course none of us had an appetite. I forced myself to take a few bites to be able to function through the next few days. I was so weak and tired from no sleep and the stress of the past 24 hours, I could barely walk or stay upright.

Our next goal was to find a place to stay, as there were four of us and my parents' place was small. We had several offers, but we needed somewhere to stay for more than just a couple days. I did not know how long or what it was going to take to make the arrangements. I had never lost anyone close to me. This was all new territory.

My old timeshare boss said he would get me a room at the resort where I used to work. It was perfect as it had a small kitchenette, separate bedroom and living room so it fit all of us nicely. We checked in, which was challenging as none of us were in a good state.

We decided to sleep before doing anything else. Some of us slept, but I couldn't. We would wake up crying and just hold each other. I don't think I could have survived this time without my family.

I made an appointment for the next morning to go pick up Cody's belongings at the coroner's office. Richard and his wife met us there. We were told we could not see his body at the coroner's, but at the funeral home after his body was sent there.

I entered the coroner's office and they handed me a black backpack. I grabbed his stuff and walked out and broke down. *This is it. This is all I have left of my beautiful boy?* My daughters and my twin held me up, as I could barely stand.

My daughters started going through his belongings. There was his wallet and a few bottles of allergy medications. There was a note I had given him a while back after his first or second psychotic break. The note read: *I love you so much dude, you're doing a great job! Have an amazing day!*

He had actually kept that in his wallet. I could barely see anything through the tears. My daughters and twin kept going through his stuff, but I didn't want to. It was just his stuff. *I want my boy, I don't want just his stuff!*

The next day Richard made an appointment at a cremation facility. I knew Cody would not want to have a big funeral or be buried. He would want everyone to celebrate his life. He had a unique view on life, death and spirituality. He attended the Mormon church, and later a non-denominational Christian church. Although he took bits and pieces from each, he did not agree with any religion and viewed them as a form of control. So I definitely did

CHAPTER 13

not want a traditional funeral. Jessica, his aunt Holly, his father, his father's wife, and I met at the cremation place.

Going out in public and interacting with people was difficult at this time. I couldn't be my normal polite, smiley self. But I also didn't feel right acting rude or somber, as that was not my natural state. I didn't know how to act in the world now. I wonder if others feel this way as they grieve? Nobody would know or care what I was going through but I just wanted to tell everyone I encountered, *I lost my son. I lost my son, and now I don't know how to live or act or just be. Please be nice to me, please be gentle.* But of course I couldn't say that to everyone I met or else I'd probably end up in a psychiatric hospital. So I acted somewhere in between normal and a lost, grieving mother.

Richard was not very present during our visit to the cremation place, so I answered most of the questions. The information on the death certificate ended up all wrong. My husband's first name was with my maiden name. Clearly I was not in my right mind. I wished someone else would make all of these decisions for me. *I don't want to be doing any of this. Can't someone else just do this for me!?* I had never lost anyone so I didn't know what to do. Now

I realize how important it is for someone to be there for you when you grieve, to help make all of these decisions.

Several days passed and Cody's friends asked when the services would be. But there were no services. His body was just going to be cremated. I felt like we should do something to honor his life and gather all of those that loved him. One of his friends said they were going to go up to the mountains where they found his body. This gave me the idea to have a candlelight vigil up on the mountain where his life ended. Cody loved the mountains and would go up there often to meditate. My twin sister, my daughters and I planned the vigil and posted it on social media. Several of Cody's friends from Utah drove down for it.

We went up prior to the vigil and had a few of his friends from Utah join us at the lodge to eat. Knowing this was the last place my son was alive hit me like a ton of bricks. I sobbed wanting one last time to hold him, smell him, and see his huge smile. *Why, why, why?* is all I could think.

But honestly, I knew why.

From the day Cody was born, his life was challenging. He was never comfortable in his skin. His thoughts were never at peace, and his soul was on fire on this earth. I wanted him here for my own selfish reasons, but I know this world was not the place for him. He was now free from the chains of his body, his addiction and his illness. I know deep in my heart he fought as long as he could and now he was free. But I was left with the chain of heartache, of regret, of loss and emptiness that could never be filled.

Over thirty people showed up for the candlelight vigil. One friend showed up with a huge 2-liter bottle of Dr. Pepper and a box of cereal, two of Cody's favorite things. Viktor, a friend of Cody's that I had never met or even known of, came up to me and held me and sobbed. I knew he must've been close to Cody as he sobbed, and found myself comforting him. *How was I finding this strength? Maybe Cody gave it to me, so I could show them his strength.* Others played electronic dance music on their car speakers. His best friend, Jessica, brought Krispy Kreme donuts from where he used to work and handed them out. We all held the fake candles and stood in a circle as everyone shared their thoughts and memories of my son.

This was a life-changing experience that I cannot explain. I had no clue how many lives he touched – how many people he helped – and how many people he had made smile. I was grieving; but I also was proud to know what my son had done in his short life on this earth.

This is what his sister, Jessica, read at the candlelight vigil:

My angel. My twin. My DJ. My hero. Cody. You were an angel without wings here on earth. You truly didn't give a damn what people thought and I completely admire that about you.

These past two years were the most trying times for you and I know the things you said and did weren't your true self. You didn't mean anyone harm.

I know your beautiful soul truly was selfless, caring, nonjudgmental, and beautiful. You would give the shirt off your back, literally, to anyone who needed it. Your warm smile and infectious laugh could brighten anyone's day.

You meant the world to me. You do mean the world to me. I know you are truly my guardian angel now. Thank you for the 21 years you gave me. Thank you for the hard times and the good times. Those memories will live on in me forever. I know your home in heaven with granny now. Your legacy will be carried on through us all.

We miss you DJ CODEX

CHAPTER 13

Two months later the coroner's office called with the toxicology results. Cody's death was officially ruled a suicide from an overdose of amphetamines and Tylenol PM, along with the ingredient from Benadryl. That was not all that surprising, but what surprised me was the physical asphyxiation. His neck was basically broken after falling down the mountain. At least that was what I assumed. The image burned in my mind and I broke down. I knew he took his own life, but getting the official cause of death and saying the words, along with the physical asphyxiation, set in. I had to leave work because I could not stop crying. My baby was gone.

CELEBRATING CODY

Jessica and the Tattoo

Cody was very hesitant about getting any tattoos because he was afraid he would end up regretting them in the future. But one thing he always wanted was his DJ name tattooed on his left wrist: DJ CODEX. He would write it on his wrist in big block letters with a black sharpie almost weekly.

He never got this tattoo. So the week after we lost him I had DJ CODEX tattooed on my left wrist in Cody's handwriting. My mom, sister, cousin and aunt did the same. It is a beautiful way to remember him. I love being able to look down and see his messy handwriting on my wrist everyday.

CHAPTER 14

GRIEF – WHAT I DID NOT KNOW

I knew one day I would have to experience grief; it is part of life. But I had hoped it would not be this soon or include my child. It's not like you can grieve and then you are done grieving. Grief hits you over and over and over and over. It just keeps coming. And coming. And coming. Again and again.

Grief is not just sadness. It is multiple emotions and feelings that are unique to each individual. It was new territory for me. I had never had a devastating loss in my life up until this point. Sure, I had lost my grandparents who I loved dearly, but they had lived in Minnesota and were not in my life every day. I had lost a few aunts and uncles, which was sad, but again, I wasn't that close with them either. My parents and siblings were all still alive.

I had been through a divorce, which was a sort of loss, and I had to grieve that.

But this... this was devastating... tragic... traumatizing. This... was... *loss*. This was the type of loss that tore your heart out and left a gaping hole. This was indescribable pain. A pain I had never felt before. This was the type of loss that redirects your whole life. It changes your perspective on *everything*. It was an earthquake that levels an entire city and leaves its residents in awe of its destruction – standing hopelessly; wandering without direction; confused with despair; not knowing how to take the next step. My boy, my one and only son, my first born was gone. Not just gone; *he had taken his own life.*

So many questions loomed. After some of the dust settled, Richard went up to the mountain to retrieve the car Cody had left up there. He brought it back to his house. My twin sister Danielle and Savannah went through Cody's car. They found a big plastic bin. On it was written, "Give this bin to Lacey at Red Rock Casino Starbucks. These are our memories."

In it he had shirts and memorabilia, and a tiny safe that had a lock on it. We took the safe and some of his things back to the hotel with us. We were curious about what was in the safe, so we took a butter knife and pried it open. Inside were four cell phones. The newest one did not have a passcode on it so we could unlock it and see photos, messages and calls. Savannah found some videos. She opened the video and it was Cody sitting in his car crying with a song played in the background. *Your love is one in a million.*

He was placing things in the bin and speaking to his ex-girlfriend Lacey saying, "I have to go to the other side to help guide you."

My son took his life to help guide his girlfriend? *What*!? We were all furious. A girlfriend who wanted nothing to do with him. He took his own life to help her? But after the anger subsided, along with the devastation of learning it was suicide (instead of an accidental overdose), we thought about Cody and his nature.

Cody took his own life to help someone else. It sounds crazy; but ultimately, I came to see it as a selfless act. Yes, he had been doing drugs, was delusional and mentally unstable… but in his deranged mind, he was ultimately unselfish.

I spent two weeks in Las Vegas cleaning out his apartment and spending time with my sister and parents before flying back to Florida. The new reality and grief hit me like a ton of bricks, coming in waves and at unexpected moments. Nothing and everything triggered it.

I now know grief intimately, and it's not what I had imagined it to be. There is no end point. Nothing makes it go away. Grief is not linear, and there is no right way to grieve. I wish I did not have to know this type of grief. I never thought that I could survive losing one of my children. But I did.

I am no longer the same person I was before; the old me did not survive. She is gone, but a new person has evolved. In some ways I'm more compassionate, especially to others who have lost a child or someone close to them. I look at death and life very differently. I am not afraid to die, as I know I will be reunited with Cody when I do. I also view the afterlife differently. I believe there is a beautiful afterlife. Energy cannot be created or destroyed, it just changes form. Cody's energy changed from existing inside a body to now existing in spirit form. I feel him and sense him at times.

I know Cody chose me to be his mother. I know we made a pact before coming to earth that we were going to teach each other love, patience, forgiveness, and yes, pain. Because when you know pain, then you can truly know and appreciate love, joy and beauty. To know and appreciate the good, we must endure and experience the not so good things in life. If we only had sunlight, we would not appreciate it. So we have the dark in order to appreciate the light. We have pain to appreciate those times where there is no pain.

Now, in his death, I have come to realize what an impact Cody had on so many people. His friends and co-workers have shared such great memories, and those memories and thoughts have brought me a certain level of comfort. Knowing that his smile brought so much joy to others brings a smile to my face. He was loved, and loved deeply. He was greatly appreciated. His life and presence made a difference to others. Everyone he came in contact with remembers his big heartfelt smile... but many did not know the pain he had inside.

Grief is a way of life. Grief never goes away. It is always inside of you, despite what shows on the outside. Grief is integrated into your being and daily life. It may sound strange, but I know now that I can grieve and be happy at the same time. I can grieve and still have fun and appreciate what I have now. I can love despite the loss; and see the beauty of what is and what could be, despite my beautiful son not existing here with me to enjoy all of life's joys.

I have such amazing people in my life. I have family, friends, my parents, my sisters, and my daughters. I appreciate how much they support me and love me. But one thing I have learned is no matter how much they say or do to help me through this, nothing – absolutely nothing – can or will change the loss and grief. Grief truly is a lonely journey that each person must do on their own, in their own way, and in their own heart and mind.

What gets me through some days may not work for other people who are grieving. I must face each day on my own – and find what helps me cope. Today may not look like tomorrow in my grief journey, and next year may not look like this year. But I will continue to live each day the best I know how and with love in my heart knowing my son would only want happiness for me. He would want us all to laugh, dance and listen to music. So, that is what I will do – especially on my low days: I will turn on EDM and laugh, cry, and dance for Cody.

Everything about Cody was unique, and that included his date of birth. The significance of the date of his birth never really stood out for me before – 1.19.1999. It only occurred to me after his death. According to numerology (Cody was very into this), the number 1 is beginnings :

Angel number 1 symbolizes new beginnings. It will give you the energy to step out of your comfort zone and step into the unknown. You need to get rid of negative thoughts and look forward to a new opportunity. It's important to trust your instincts and not to be afraid of new opportunities in your life.

CHAPTER 14

And the number 9 is:

The angel number 999 is a sign to let you know that some parts of your life are coming to an end and completion.

It is interesting to think about it now: his birthdate signifies the beginning and the end. The beginning of a new life for me and an ending of a life for my son as well as an ending of my life as I knew it. I now pay close attention to numbers as my son did. I constantly see 11:11 on the clock or 3:33 and I smile and think of him. Perhaps he is sending me a message to keep going.

A week after finishing this last chapter I saw a post on Facebook from a female who was lonely and wanted to connect with people. She was living in South Africa. I will call her *Mary*. For some reason this touched my heart so I posted, "Sending you love from Florida USA."

She replied, "Thank you. I feel your love!"

A few days later I sent her a private message asking her if she would like to chat. She quickly responded and introduced herself. We chatted a bit about what we did for work and how life was over in South Africa. Then the chat took a turn.

Mary: My sympathies for your beautiful son, he is angelic.

Diana: Thank you, he is a beautiful soul, he said he had to "go to the other side to help guide" and he took his own life. I know he is at peace now.

Mary: He is at peace and his energy is very much around you.

Diana: Yes, I feel it.

Mary: Your son is guiding us all, he is assisting young ones as they die in trauma and cross through; it is beautiful but I can't help but cry. He chose a very intense path, to learn quickly so he could fulfill his mission, a great soul indeed.

Diana: Yes, he did have an intense path.

Mary: He is at peace and so are you, because you understand, he chose his mom well.

Diana: I feel like he is speaking through you.

Mary: Yes, I just didn't want to say it. He is here comforting me. He's very adept at healing the heart. I am in grief too as my mom is passing.

Diana: Oh, thank you, Cody, thank you – that is beautiful, yes.

Mary: You guys laughed a lot and cried a lot, he thanks you for the emotion. He learned so much about the heart; He was always in his heart, seldom in his body, if that makes sense. He's having a blast.

Diana: Aww that's beautiful, I'm crying.

Mary: He loves being free of the body, but hovers over you. He wants you to know, it's all good.

Diana: Yes, my son I know.

Mary: He says, "I love you mom, always. Don't miss me so much, I'm right here." (She says) Wow I have hectic energy chills, he is strong.

Diana: Oh yes, yes.

Mary: An elderly female was with him as he stepped out; he was not alone, dude, this is strange.

Diana: It's Grandma Penny!!

Mary: The lady looks like Dolores Cannon (an author of the Facebook page we both follow and where we connected).

Diana: She passed 5 months prior to Cody.

Mary: Yes, yes, yes, yes! My whole body is reacting. Penny passed to be there waiting to guide him through. She says, "I love you" to you. She's with him, so much love and happiness. They want you to fully understand, he says again, "It's all good, mom." He's showing thumbs up. They are free and doing their cosmic service. Now he puts two thumbs up.

I was bawling. This hit me hard out of nowhere. I had the chills the whole time she was messaging me. I feel it really was Cody talking through her. Perhaps it was wishful thinking, but whether or not you believe in channeling, or a spirit's ability to send messages from the spirit world, it brought me peace. Even a little peace in this grieving process, is a welcomed thing. I never heard from *Mary* again.

AFTERWARD
WRITING

I was not able to save my son. Even though I work in the mental health field and have multiple degrees in clinical psychology, and even though I applied my knowledge and experience to help him, I was not able to save him.

As the old saying goes, "You can lead a horse to water but you can't make it drink." My son did not want help. In his mind he was fine – it was the rest of the world that was wrong. Part of me now believes this too. He lived his life on his terms and was authentically and unapologetically himself. He was different and beautiful and loving and kind and mean and scary – he was all these things. But he was my beautiful boy. A life gone too soon. My heart and soul will forever be missing a part of it.

I thought the parent was supposed to teach the child. In my case, my son taught me much of what I know today. He taught me to love, to live, to laugh, to be true to myself – to dance even if I am scared – to not apologize for being me.

Cody's was a short life, but length does not always correspond to impact. I hope that our story has helped you to understand your own self or others who may struggle with the same issues my son did. Sharing this story is also a way to heal, for it is only in complete honesty that we can heal.

This book was divinely guided – by my son, by spirit guides, by God or something of that nature – because it came to me fairly easily. I also believe my son knew this would be therapeutic for me, and would help me heal. The idea to write this book came to me in a hotel room in Las Vegas when I was with my daughters and my twin sister just days after Cody died. I had never thought of this before, and certainly never imagined this is what I would do or where my life would take me. The idea just magically popped in my head and I said out loud, "I'm going to write a book about Cody!"

So a couple months after I returned to my home in Florida, each Saturday or Sunday morning I would go off by myself for several hours and write. My goal was to write at least one chapter a weekend. I would go sit on the beach or at a park, and the thoughts would just flow out of me without much effort.

I work in the mental health field and plan to donate many books to mental health clinics so that those who are living with mental illness, or their family members, can read this and know they are not alone. Hopefully our story will give others who are fighting this ugly fight the hope to keep going.

To those fighting through mental illness, addiction or thoughts of suicide – you are brave. Mental illness and addiction are like trying to survive a storm – a storm that has you hanging on to a tree branch out in the elements, and the wind and water just keep beating on you. Cody was brave for 22 years. The fact that you get up each day, as my son did, makes you a warrior! There is help! Get treatment. Do not remain in the dark.

For those facing challenges or loss, perhaps the only thing you might find on those hard days is the beauty of the warm sun on your face; a smile from a stranger; a child running by you laughing and playing. But when you are ready for it, you will find you are surrounded by beauty. But only you can determine when you are ready. Nobody can force you to be ready. You have to be willing to choose it, to see it. Be gentle with yourself. Be kind. Be forgiving – because the journey of grief is long and lonely.

ACKNOWLEDGMENTS

It takes a village to raise a child and these are the people in my village who helped me to raise Cody: my twin sister, Danielle Harding; my daughters Jessica and Savannah Ward; my two older sisters, Denise and Debra; and my beautiful parents Bob and Beverly Harding. I am so grateful that you raised me to be the resilient person that I am.

Also, to my son's father, his family, and all my amazing friends along the way who have given me support, comfort, and love through this tragedy, but have allowed me to grieve in the way that I needed. Thank you to my Park Royal Hospital family, Dr. Asaaf Aleem, Amber Hentz, Youselande Devariste, Jennifer Brady, and Meaghan Palumbo. Thank you.

REFLECTIONS

Jessica, Sister

When I am sad and start missing Cody I remember the night he came to sit with me when I was upset and I told him the story of the girl with cerebral palsy, because it just shows that he was an angel on earth. He felt with such a crazy amount of emotion for everyone he came across. He was too sensitive and unique to be on this earth. I just hope he is at peace and feels endless love.

It's such a strange feeling losing someone so special, because part of me just aches to touch him again, and the other part is at ease knowing he isn't tortured on this hell we call earth, anymore.

James Jordan, After School Program Director

Heaven gained such a creative and loving soul. Cody, I'll see ya down the road and on the other side.

Dallas Lowry, Wrestling Coach

Cody touched many lives with his angelic smile. When his classmates and coworkers shared their thoughts and memories I realized how big an impact he had on others. I always knew he was special. He wasn't meant to just "fit in." He never felt like he did. But that is how he was meant to be in order to stand out and touch so many lives with his spirit.

RESOURCES

If you or someone you know is having thoughts of suicide or is in crisis, help is available. Call or text 988 or chat 988lifeline.org

SUICIDE HOTLINE 988

National Institute of Mental Health:
https://www.nimh.nih.gov/

National Alliance on Mental Health:
800-950-6264
https://www.nami.org

Suicide Prevention Resource Center:
https://sprc.org/

Substance Abuse and Mental Health Administration:
https://www.samhsa.gov/find-help/national-helpline

ABOUT THE AUTHOR
DIANA WARD

Born in San Diego, California, Diana's family moved to Las Vegas, Nevada, in 1988, where she spent most of her adult life. Diana had a successful career in real estate; but after the real estate crash of 2008, she had to reinvent herself and find a new career path. After losing her home, car and life's savings, she moved to southern Utah and decided to go to college at the age of 37 – as a single mother with three young children. Diana attended Southern Utah University in Cedar City, Utah, where she found her passion for psychology and understanding human behavior. She obtained a bachelor's degree in psychology and returned to Las Vegas for employment. She then obtained her master's degree in health psychology. Diana has a passion for understanding how the body and mind connect.

Immediately after receiving her master's degree she began working at an inpatient psychiatric hospital as a social worker, and has a strong desire to help those with mental health and addiction issues. In 2019, Diana enrolled in a PhD program in clinical psychology.

The tragic loss of her son sent Diana on a new life mission of raising awareness on mental health, addiction and suicide. Diana now lives in southwest Florida with her two daughters and two sisters, where she continues to work in the inpatient psychiatric setting that treats acute psychiatric issues as well as substance abuse detox and long-term treatment. She is passionate about breaking the stigma of mental health issues, as well as raising awareness to prevent others from reaching the point that her son did when he decided to take his own life. With *Behind the Smile* she plans to reach as many families and individuals as possible to help prevent another statistic of loss.

www.ingramcontent.com/pod-product-compliance
Lightning Source LLC
Chambersburg PA
CBHW061808070526
44586CB00024B/2764